AVAD

TO SERVE

With love and appreciation

Ray Gimenez

6 - 26 - 20

Thank you!

Col 3:23

Ray Gimenez

Prepared for Publication By

PUBLISHING

MAKING YOUR BOOK A REALITY

843-929-8768 | info@BandBpublishingLLC.com

CONTENTS

INTRODUCTION

AVAD

You will learn to identify where you are out of step with God's plan for your life and how to get back in step

AVAD - This Hebrew word means to serve, but it also means to work, and even to worship. This word has some interesting implications for our daily lives. Unless we are in ministry, we tend to think of our jobs as secular work. However, we should consider our secular work equivalent with our service for God, which is the way we worship Him. We need to realize that all our working in our lives is for the serving of God. Every aspect of our lives is a work and witness to the great God we serve.

This book is dedicated to those who hunger and thirst for righteousness, to those who want to serve God better, to those who want to be mature in Him.

"Whatever you do, work at it with all your heart, as working for the Lord, not for men."
Colossians 3:23

Apostle Ray L. Gimenez serves as President and founder of Victory Center Ministries in Clinton Iowa. Born in Havana Cuba, Ray came to the United States with his parents in 1961 and settled in the Bronx NYC. He was a first round baseball pick in 1971 for the Detroit Tigers and after 5 years in the minor leagues, he pursued a career in ministry. In 1987 he founded Victory Center an emergency homeless shelter for men, women, and families. He served Open Bible Churches for 6 years as the National Director of Hispanic Ministries. He has been instrumental in empowering many men & women to the pastoral ministry has traveled extensively to 23 countries holding crusades and serves in the Advisory Board of the International Coalition of Apostles (ICAL). Ray is married to Mary Anne, both of Clinton and together they have 11 children and 23 grandchildren.

CHAPTER 1

PERSONAL TESTIMONY:
UNDERSTANDING FEAR

When I was ten years old and my brother Isaac was 8, both of us were on the floor underneath our bed, we heard shots...BANG! BANG! Then an explosion, then another! We heard the cries, the screaming of wounded people. The more sounds we heard the more profound was the fear that grew in our hearts!

It was 1960 in the country of Cuba. Fidel Castro had gathered his revolutionaries and attacked innocent families that were opposing his communistic regime. We had been told by our parents to take refuge underneath our beds...so we obeyed! Fear had entered our hearts and fear was our way of life. In those days my family had very little options to survive. We opposed the communistic government way of life, so we were oppressed hastily by Castro's men. Our parent's jobs were confiscated. My brother, Isaac, and I were kicked out of the school system. Our family would now survive by the generosity of our family line and friends. Fear to survive was a daily application. The tenacity of my parents allowed us to reverse fear with a win at an all cost attitude. Daily we visited friends of the family and they always had something to eat for my younger brother Isaac, Lili, and myself. Our goal was to reverse the fear and the terrorist's tactics of the Government with FAITH.

FEAR A SPIRITUAL FORCE.

2 Timothy 5:7 says, "God has not given us the spirit of fear." Fear is not one of God's attributes. Notice that the Bible calls it a Spirit. If it's not part of God's spirit, then it must be Satan's. As living agents of Christ we must understand the powerful tool Satan uses against the people of God. He strikes fear in the heart of men to cause men's hearts to fail, to detain them from their goal, and to destroy their ability to connect with God. These 3 major principles are deployed in the strategies mind of Satan's demonic forces to render God's people helpless in their work for God and to strike fear in the hearts of men.

Mom and Dad were now without jobs, without the dignity of having their sons in public or private school were in fear. At this time in Cuba we resorted to depend on friends and family members for survival. We lived one day at a time...Today I have an old saying, "Life by the yard is hard...Life by the inch is a cinch." Maybe I learned this principle early on because of how we lived in our homeland.

It was an embarrassing moment for my parents to have to pursue food and nutrition for their children from others. But the situation got worse...Castro's government made a law that anyone not being in their homes by a certain time was risking a communistic seal in their house which meant the Government then had control of your home and all your belongings. One day in the spring of 1961, the family was out after this communistic time curfew due the hardship of not having enough to eat. We had gone to a friend's home to pick up a hot meal for the family, and when we came back immediately we noticed the red seal on our door. Mom was devastated; she began to cry out... Our dwelling place was now also confiscated by the communistic Government of Cuba. Physically we were fearful, stressed, depressed, and full of remorse. How are we to survive? Heart trouble continues to comprise around the world as the number one reason people die. Heart ailment is attributed to the hardening of the arteries to the heart. It is caused by sickness, worry, depression and yes, fear.

BE STRONG

In Satan's arsenal, fear ranks way up there as a primary weapon. When Moses died and the mantle was passed to Joshua, the first words given by God to Joshua was "Be strong and Courageous" (Joshua 1:6). If fear is a spiritual force used by Satan then we must reverse this with faith. God says to Joshua as he's saying to all of us today, "Be strong, activate your faith, be courageous." In other words do not fear. A good way I look at it now is this way...when I have an absence of fear then my faith which is a spiritual force by God that keeps me in victory. Not being Christians in Cuba, fear began to consume my mother. Dad was in New York City working in a factory and we were homeless in Cuba due to the communists hardship placed on us. We managed to live in our grandfather's apartment in Ronda 15 which is an apartment house across from the University of Habana. Mom thought we would be isolated and killed because of our opposition to Castro's Government. But we pressed on!! And finally after the checks came in from Dad's work in NYC, our paperwork was ready to be presented to the Cuban Embassy. We were cleared to come to the United States and so we left Habana. Mom, my brother Isaac, my sister Lili and I on August 20th, 1961.

Upon arriving in Miami, we did not have the funds to take us to New York City, so we slept at the Airport. The Catholic Church had a program to help the Cuban refugees, so they bought our tickets.

NEW YORK CITY

As we got off the plane, it become immediately apparent that we were facing a culture shock. Where were the beaches? Where are the palm branches? The Hispanic people, where were they? The language barrier a huge problem.

TRANSITION A GOOD THING

Becoming a Christian for the first time is also a culture shock in some ways. My initial experience coming into New York City relates to my initial born again experience.

Where are my friends? Where are the people I hung out with? The Christian language is completely different than that of the world. That's why we read in 2 Cor 5:17, "old things are passed away, behold all things become new." Many people do not want to follow you because you're a new person.

Transitioning to a brand-new life with Christ is a good thing. We don't even talk the same when we become all that Christ wants to do in our lives. There is a language barrier! This transition from one country to another allowed me to meet new friends, experience new relationships. In my Christian life it was the same, and it was fun!

At age 11 you pick up languages rapidly. However, it was not the same for my mom & dad in their 30's? Working in a factory was the best they could do in New York City to alleviate their sense of worth. They began drinking alcohol on the weekends; however, it was one fight after another. Alcohol has an evil ingredient that can poison your life standards. The devil will use any method to destroy your life and happiness and certainly drinking is one of them. I began to realize in the short time we were in NYC that the environment was mostly evil. Drugs where everywhere, violence, gangs, filth of every measure...It was the slumps in the Bronx where we first lived. Thieves broke in to steal; rats and roaches infested our 5th floor apartment. We lived in a squalid condition in just 2 small bedrooms. We had our grandparents who later exiled from Cuba also living there, then later an uncle and aunt and before too long 12 people living in a small 2-bedroom apartment. The thought of hopelessness filled our refugee family. Thoughts of going back to our homeland Cuba was disappearing as Castro's revolutionaries began to stabilize their communistic regime. I felt the obligation as a first born to rescue my struggling family, but first I must overcome threats in the NYC school system and overcome the spirit of fear. There are different forms that the spirit of fear will use against you. Here is a good list linked to holding you back: Fear of high places (acrophobia), fear of lighting (astraphobia), fear of enclosed places (claustrophobia), fear of water (hydrophobia), fear of darkness (nyctophobia), fear of fire (pyrophobia), fear of death (phanatobia), we must learn to overcome them to move forward.

THREATENED BUT READY TO FIGHT

The first snow hit in the winter of 1961 and as an 11-year-old my brother and I thought the world had come to an end. Cuba's climate is about 75 degrees year around so here we were at 25 degrees wearing thin sweaters. My father recognized the need for coats, so he took us down to the Salvation Army in the Bronx. And bought two real heavy trench coats they reached up to our ankles. We wore those to school, and we were made fun of. We looked like a couple of penguins walking down the North Pole. This toppled by our language barrier, Isaac and I could not be ridiculed enough. Then there was the school bully Tony, who would steal my lunch in my little bag quite regularly. He also threatens to beat me up if I told anyone. Regularly he would see me coming down the school hallway and send my books flying and take my lunch bag. I got so used to this that I learned to hide from him if I saw him afar off.

One day I was watching Cassius Clay on TV, (now called Muhamad Ali), he was then the world champion of boxing. I heard him mouth these words: I'll fly like a butterfly, and sting like a bee." Something inside of me said..."hey I could be like him...a champion!" I could fly like a butterfly and sting like a bee! So, I went to my mirror and I began to practice my jabs and punches, and footwork. Pretty soon I got enough courage to say to myself "I could beat this bully and become the champion."

By now if you're reading this testimony you figured out what I am going to say next. The devil will mock you and make fun of you and threaten to beat you up. He will take your self-worth and throw it in a gutter somewhere. Yes, he will do this regularly unless you can convince yourself that you are more powerful than him. With Christ in you the devil is the one that will suffer loss. You can become unstoppable if you rely on God's strength. Here's the lesson I learned! I have applied this to my life in every hardship...

"He will deliver you out of all your troubles."
Psalm 34:17

After I made my mind up to challenge this bully, I went to school full of confidence. I said to myself I will not run and hide; I will face him! Sure enough, here Tony came walking toughly down the hallway. He looked at me as he had many times before and proceeded to knock my books down. After I picked them up, I pushed him as hard as I could. Staring me in the face he said "wait for me at 3'o clock in the front of the school yard. I knew this meant the fight was on! I quickly added "I'll be there"! By noon the entire school knew about the fight except of course the teachers and the principal. As 2PM came around my confidence had diminished somewhat. But I knew I could not back down...I was fighting for my family, my reputation and for many friends who were abused by this bully. Life as a Christian is a fight to the finish. Despite my fear I resolved to take the risk of getting beat up. After all, this bully was much stronger than I and had more experience in fighting. Many of us have to face our Goliath daily and we must determine to fight even if it means you might lose. Your family is at risk; your reputation can be tarnished if you back down. Your friends will disown you for your cowardice ways. You must fight; you must see yourself as a winner!

SEE YOURSELF AS A WINNER

Romans 4:17 says "call those things that are not as though they were." This simply means you must see yourself winning despite the odds. The winners never quit; they hang around even after the storm clears. I know now but I did not know then that God and I are a majority over everything in life. When the 3'oclock bell rang I walked slowly but confidently to the front of the school yard. I had become confident again because I saw images of me fighting this bully flying like a butterfly and stinging like a bee. I saw me victorious! A champion like Cassius

Clay! To my surprise it seemed like the whole school went out to witness this fight in the school yard. Tony flexed his muscles as I entered the area of the event. I was just a scrawny little Cuban boy, so I did not want to flex my muscles and embarrass myself. So, I proceeded to fly like a butterfly around him hitting him with the quick jabs that I had practiced in the mirror the night before. Every time I landed one somewhere on his face the crowd cheered! It was as though they were cheering for the underdog! I dodged a few of his hard punches and continued to land jabs across his face, (however not hard at all). I could see that he was becoming frustrated, frustrated that the crowd was not on his side, frustrated perhaps because he could not land his heavy artillery. The devil also gets frustrated when we as Christians dodge his attacks through faith and perseverance. And he gets really mad when he cannot land a punch! If we hide his word in our heart, he can't land anything. Finally, after dancing and jabbing Tony's frustration reached the max! He decided not to fight like boxers but wrestle! He leaped upon me and wrestled me to the ground. He had me in a headlock; it was then that I decided that with my free hands to start hitting him on the head... I was not going to quit! I was in it too far now! Just as I began to hit him, being under a head lock, someone lifts my body off the ground by my ear...it was the principal of the school! He had Tony's ear too. The principal took us both to his office and suspended us from school for fighting. Tony and I were sweating. We were sitting down in the chairs awaiting the pink slip the principal was writing. I looked at Tony and he looked like a whipped puppy! I quickly noticed he had a little blood gushing out of his forehead. I then took my hands and felt all over my face to see if I had blood gushing out somewhere. When my hands showed no sign of blood, in my mind I declared myself the winner, the champion! Despite the suspension I felt honorable, a young boy with some dignity...I have won the fight! After this episode Tony became good friends with me, the old saying "If you can't beat him join him." The good part of this season of my life is simply this...we sometimes need to fight to bring peace to your life. Spiritual warfare says I will fight with the enemy until he is defeated. Luke 10:19 tells us that "God has given us power over all the works of the enemy." We need to use the weapon of faith against our adversary his fear tactics will not work then, he will be disarmed. The victory is yours when we activate faith. 2 Timothy 1:7 says "He has not given us the spirit of fear." So let's not use it.

INFLUENCED BY THE YANKEES

The word influence is a spiritual warfare word. We need to pray like Jabez prayed in the Old Testament. "Oh Lord extend my territory!" (2 Chronicles). The devil's arsenal includes detaining, destroying, and disarming your Christian influence. If he can slow you down by applying stress, fear, sickness, and financial hardships then he's won. All of us as Human beings are influenced by someone. Isaiah's first cousin was King Uzziah...Isaiah begins his testimony in Chapter 6 of his book by these words: "In the year that King Uzziah died." Personally, as the love of baseball grew in my heart in the city of New York I was fond of the great Yankee teams of the 60's. They influenced my life greatly! I wanted to be a winner like them. I wanted to play for them someday. Watching the likes of Mickey Mantle, Roger Maris, and Whitey Ford was a huge thrill for me. This passion for the game propelled me to study the game of baseball and it provided a dream to enhance the lives of my parents. I was influenced by the Yankees, so I went for it. At age 13 I began to play in the pony leagues, then onto 4 teams at the same time in the summer. Being influenced by the game of baseball kept me away from drugs, alcohol, and crime. I made the varsity team at Theodore Roosevelt in the Bronx as a Freshman, captain as a Sophomore, and tied with votes for the all city shortstop in NYC as a Senior.

THE GOAL HELP'S THE FAMILY

I had my mind made up to succeed in the game of Baseball. My goal was clear to make enough money to help my mom and dad get out of the slumps of NYC. I wanted them to be able to purchase a car, take a vacation. To do this I needed a vigorous exercise and practice system to be able to excel. To be a top-notch Christian you need to have some work ethics. You must have a system routine in place. Prayer, Bible study, fellowship with other believers, church attendance. Anyone of these not being there can cause the enemy to come in and stop your Christian influence. Realizing the need to excel in the game of Baseball I set up my system. Run 5 miles a day, swing the bat 300 times, play in the school yards hitting the ball daily at least a couple hundred times.

The abuse of alcoholism took a different toll in my family. Mom and Dad both lost their interest in following my young Baseball career due to their abuse of alcohol. Every weekend all-nighter led to many fights and stress and economic hardships. This lifestyle was the component the enemy used to have them ignore the way I was excelling in the game of Baseball. Mom and Dad never saw me play, not one Pony League game or High School game. In their minds they were determined that I as their oldest son should study and become a Lawyer, as a matter of fact they insisted.

DRIVEN BY PASSION

I was motivated to excel in the game of baseball only because I wanted to help my parents end their economic hardships. But in my favor, I developed a strong love and passion for the game of baseball. It kept me from using drugs, alcohol, and being in street gangs. And yes I was offered numerous times to try these things but I was never driven to do them because of two motivating factors: my love for my parents and my love for the game. This passion kept me from the temptations of trying drugs, alcohol and gangs. The enemy is clever if you don't have a passion to serve Christ he will undoubtedly try to place a passion to serve him with lust, and wild living. When that happens, we easily give in because we don't have the true passion for the Lord.

Keeping your eyes on him and loving him will keep you in the right path 100% of the time. Even though I was not a Christian my passion for the game of baseball kept me away from all the evil. So, I have come to a conclusion if it works in the natural it will work even better in the supernatural. So I keep the central scripture of the Bible in the center of all I do:

> *"Love me with all your heart, with all your soul, and with all your mind...For this is the first commandment." (Matthew 22:37).*

DRAFTED

I know that the Lord chooses us for specific assignments in life. For his purposes He places divine anointing's or gifting's upon our lives. There's always work we need to do for Him. The Bible says he chose us. He has added unto us the ministry of reconciliation. He said we are to bear fruit in his name. In other words, God drafts us to work some jobs, but it all depends on the anointing, the talents he places on us. It's all for His pleasure and purposes. Our job is to serve him. Evident of this is the parable of the talents. To one he gave (5) to another he gave (2) and to another he gave (1). I believe he gives us abilities to handle specific things. The story of the talents shows that the two who doubled the talents were rewarded, but the one who buried his talent was condemned. So, it is with anyone who wastes their life in wild living and does not use God's created gift for his purposes.

FOURTH PICK FOR THE DETROIT TIGERS

In 1971, I was selected (drafted) in the first round 4th pick overall from the Detroit Tigers, having hit a ton of homeruns for the Brooklyn Community College Baseball team in New York City. I was headed to Lakeland Florida to begin my professional Baseball career. I was sent to Bristol Virginia before all of this. I wanted to fulfill my first dream which was to help Mom and Dad. I decided to give them my entire signing bonus minus a thousand dollars which I saved for my expenses. Mom and Dad were thrilled! They took the money and bought their first car, took their first ever vacation and moved out of the slumps of New York City. I was indeed a very proud man, one of my goals was fulfilled. Goals are so important in life it keeps us focus. God wants us to have goals, the Bible says without a vision people perish. In (Habakkuk 2:2) it says, "write the vision on a tablet and keep it plain." I do not know who said it but here's one of my old sayings that I have lived by: "It is better to aim at the moon and miss it, than to aim at nothing and hit it." So, Hey! I am a pro-player now maybe not a major leaguer, but that goal will be my next chapter.

CHAPTER 2

ARRIVE AT GOD'S TIME: DEVOLOPING GREATNESS

ON THE WAY TO THE MAJOR LEAGUES

PERFECTING THE GAME - REFLECTING CHRISTIANITY

My first homerun in a professional Baseball game came in June of 1971 and what a thrill it was, to get the slap on your behind as you rounded the third base and then get congratulated by your teammates. I felt I belonged! So it is when we do something well and exciting for the Lord. It's a feeling of belonging, belonging to the greatest team in all of History, the Bible calls it a cloud of witnesses. (Hebrews 12:) It was rookie manager Jim Leyland who slapped my behind as I was rounding third base. I truly loved playing and performing for him. Leyland demanded perfection from all of his players. He taught us to treat the game well and prepare for every game to win the contest. Today Jesus is my manager, He's my commander and chief. I have learned to trust in Him and play this game we call life with all of my heart and prepare to win every contest against obstacles, against conflicts, against hardships with Him as your head coach.

To get to the major leagues as a 4th draft pick the Detroit Tigers had a road map for their investment. There were four levels to overcome each one more difficult than the latter. Level 1: rookie ball, level 2: Class A ball, Level 3: double A Ball, Level 4: Triple A Ball. You must do well in one level before you can proceed to the next level. But so it is with us with the Lord. There are four levels according to the Bible that we must all accomplish to arrive at God's very best for you. Let me explain.

LEVEL ONE - FIRST BASE

Accept the Lord Jesus Christ into your heart! Romans 10:9-10 says it this way: "If you confess with your mouth the Lord Jesus Christ and believe in your heart that God raised him from the dead, you will be saved. For it is with your mouth that your confession is made unto salvation and it's with the heart man believes unto righteousness." After your salvation, get yourself a Bible and feed your spirit man with His word. Follow and obey His word and watch what happens. It will impress you!

LEVEL TWO - SECOND BASE

Prayer is a spiritual weapon and if you're disciplined in this area you will advance to your next season. Jesus said it this way. "If you seek me first and my kingdom, I will add everything you need into your life" (Matthew 6:33). I will speak about this in more detail in another chapter.

LEVEL THREE - THIRD BASE

Fellowshipping with others, specifically with those of the household of faith is healthy for your spiritual maturity. In Hebrews the author puts it this way: "Do not neglect the assembly of believers together" (Hebrews 10:25). I grew in the Lord mightily because I put the church attendance above playing or watching a baseball game. Jesus gave this command "By this shall all men know that you're my disciples by the love you have for one another." (John 13:35).

LEVEL FOUR - HOME

Witnessing and telling your story of how God brought you out from darkness to light is how you score a homerun for your team. Jesus said, "go and make disciples" (Matthew 28:19). "Go and make disciples in Jerusalem, Judea, Samaria and the uttermost part of the world". (Acts 1:8).

I came to the Lord in Clinton, Iowa in 1973. As I commemorate my 46 years as a Christian, I have come to realize that the Christian Life is like that of a butterfly. The caterpillar hatches from its egg under the leaf of a milkweed plant...crawls around for a couple of weeks then emerges into a beautiful butterfly. Through the process called metamorphosis it then is filled with energy for sustainment by sipping nectar from flowers. I have come to understand that these four levels are Gods Restoration System. We hatch through a process called Born Again. We emerge through a process called transformation. We become beautiful by nourishing ourselves with God's word.

THE CALL TO GREATNESS

The Chicago Cubs called the "lovable losers" had not won a World Championship in 108 years. But then the year 2016 came, they were declared the World Champions of Baseball that year. Little notice was placed upon their opponent the Cleveland Indians who had not won a Championship since 1948, that's 68 years. Because of my love for the game of baseball I am acutely familiar with the feel and smell of the atmosphere of the greatest games to be played as if it were a part of me. I couldn't help but recognize the adrenaline in the Baseball diamond watching that first series game on TV. I loved it. To say that enthusiasm and passion dominates the mood would be an understatement. It was a battle of the great teams competing to become the greatest. They were 50 men (25 on each team) men with a quest –men with a goal, and that specific goal was nothing short of declaring to the entire world their greatness.

Women fantasize about relationships; men fantasize about greatness. I must admit as a man I crave significance, influence and impact. The desire I have for greatness shows up when I play a friendly game of softball or basketball. A woman might enjoy a movie with a nice soft romance story line, but men, most men, want war. I admit I love the movies with a battle, a fight, a superhero, my wife on the other hand she loves the slow pace of a western movie with horses, and cows and sheep and dogs. Moses according to Numbers 12:3, tells us that "he was a weak man". Yet Moses, the meekest man during his time, lead one of the bravest and greatest flights to freedom. Moses was able to submit himself to God's authority. God was able to do great things in him and through him. God made Moses a great man. Yet Moses was considered meek because he was willing to serve the purposes of God to reflect the Glory of God, rather than his own.

GOD WANTS YOU TO BE GREAT

In Genesis 18:17-18, God refers to Abraham as not only a great man but also a great nation. He says in that passage that "all the nations of the earth will be blessed". Earlier in Genesis 12:2 God said directly to Abraham, "I bless you, and make your name great." He said something similar to David in 2 Samuel 7:9. "I have been with you wherever you have gone and have cut off all your enemies from before you; and I will make you a great name, like the names of the great men who are on earth." Now if you're saying well that's not me. I am just an ordinary person. Well you're wrong! John 14:12 says it this way, "truly, truly I say to you, He who believes in me, the works that I do, he will also do; and greater works than these he will do." This is a pretty straight forward truth. Jesus said plainly that, if you believe in Him, you are going to do stuff that even He didn't get to do on earth. That is a powerful reality! That is a kingdom truth. Not only will you do great things that Jesus did, but you will do greater things. For instance, my ministry has several facilities housing men, women, children and families. Jesus never did that. Jesus never traveled more than a few hundred miles from the place of his birth during His earthly ministry. Yet the gospel has been spread around the world by men & women who have gone on to do greater works on earth. So, if Jesus said that you will do "Greater Works" than He did, then evidently God does not have a problem with greatness. Neither does he have a problem with the recognition of greatness, as we saw earlier when He said He would make both Abraham's and David's names great. Anytime God makes a name great, that means He is recognizing greatness.

CAUTION ABOUT GREATNESS

What you never want to do in your desire to be great is to try to steal or use up God's Glory. That is a critical principle. To do so is to follow in the footsteps of Pharaoh. You remember what Pharaoh said when Moses told Pharaoh that God had sent Moses to let God's people go. Pharaoh said no. What He was really saying. "This is my job, my career, my financial well-being at stake, and I call the shots here. I'm in charge." Pharaoh was unwilling to submit himself to divine authority and God ultimately reduced him to nothing through the plagues because He had the wrong approach to greatness. So do not let a Pharaoh mentality come into your desire for greatness. Remember there's nothing wrong wanting to be great, in fact when James and John, known as the sons of Thunder, sought a place of honor in Christ Kingdom, the other Disciples gave them a difficult time for expressing their desire for significance. However, Jesus never corrected them only for how they wanted to go about accomplishing it. Jesus didn't tell these men not to wish to be great. He didn't tell them not to desire significance, influence, and the ability to make a lasting impact. Jesus told them not to try to get it the same way that the Gentiles did. (Matthew 20:25-26) The Gentiles exercised greatness through lording it over others. They displayed their greatness in power plays and politics, much like the World today. We live in a power-driven world. Men rule by intimidation, fear-tactics, and leverage.

GREATNESS: A POSITION TO WIN FOR THE TEAM

The World Series of 2016 saw the Chicago Cubs and the Cleveland Indians go right down to the wire to the seventh game. If you were a Chicago Cubs fan ahead in the 8th inning by 3 runs with only 6 more outs to be World Champions you were feeling pretty good. Then the inevitable happened a double brought in one run and the batter for Cleveland, Rajal Davis, smashes a two-run home run to tie the game. Cubs fans which I am one of them were feeling disheartening..." Oh no, not again." However, if you were an Indians fan, Rajal Davis was your hero at the moment. You were feeling mighty fine...The game was won in extra inning by the Cubs 8-7...Rajal Davis enjoyed the power he felt when he had it, his moment served the greater need of his team. The Cubs won and Ben Zobrist received the most valuable player when he too hit a key double to drive in a run in the 10th inning. Both players did great things on Baseball's biggest stage, the World Series. Both wanted to be known by their contribution to the team. The greatest player on any team, whether a corporate, family, ministry, or sports team, is the player who makes certain that his contribution best fits within the goals and strategies of the team. That doesn't mean that he or she can't stand out for this or her accomplishments. It simply means that whatever he does must be done in unity with and in service of the greater good. Greatness is not just a position or a title, but how that position or title plays out in conjunction with the overall goal. Think about the moon; it has no light of its own. What we see when we witness the grandeur of the moon at night is simply a reflection of the light of the sun. Jesus said, "I did not come to be served, but to serve and to give my life as a ransom for many." (Matthew 20:28). In other words, your greatness ought to be making the lives within your sphere of influence better, not worse. Your greatness ought to inspire other people because they see your impact for good in the lives of others.

CHAPTER 3

THE REAL MEANING OF TIME: MOVING WITH GOD

TIME: A RULING FORCE

We need to develop a discipline to understand time. We refer to time in numerous expressions and figures of speech. We have determined that time escapes us and we have a lack of it. Consider some of the statements we make:

- "You're wasting time."
- "I do not have enough hours in a day."
- "Time is of the essence."
- "In the nick of time."
- "Time is money."

At times I feel manipulated by time. I have felt that

my present would control my future. However, we need to understand that the Lord is the creator of time, who transcends and enters time to commune with his children so they may efficiently walk in time with him. He will cause man, his most precious and most magnificent creation, to walk without fear in victory.

We wonder through life and really don't understand why we do what we do each day. We don't expect God to do anything for us. But God said..." Ask, and it will be given to you; seek and you will find; knock, and it will be opened to you. For everyone who asks receives and he who seeks finds, and to him who knocks it will be opened". (Matthew 7:7-8).

I was diagnosed with prostate cancer. The spirit of fear came upon me. I began to think I was going to die soon. This is always the enemy's way to enter into our emotions. However, I determined that I needed to ask, seek, and knock on Jesus' door. I went through a season of trauma, but God's power allowed me to experience the healing as I waited the results of the biopsy in another time frame.

ALL THE DAYS OF GOD

God is not in time. His being does not consist of moments following one another. If a thousand people are praying to him at 9A.M., we call it 9A.M. but to him it is always the present, all the days are "now" for him. He does not remember you doing things yesterday; He simply sees you doing them, because though you have lost yesterday, He has not.

By considering this characteristic of God you will realize that your Heavenly Father has access to every moment in your life from beginning to end as though they were present. With the Holy Spirit, you can actually access those times in your past when you felt betrayed, abused, abandoned, happy, fulfilled, or any other emotion or condition. You can be forgiven for the past and also travel back in time with God, see him as a "very present help" (Psalms 46:1). He can redeem those times from the past that the enemy wanted to use for evil.

After living all my childhood with alcoholic parents, a wonderful blessing happened. God used me to lead them to Christ therefore redeeming ("buying back") a season of my life. This is one of the functions of the power of salvation and deliverance: redeeming the past from the hand of the enemy so it is no longer a weapon against us. "Before we fell from grace in the garden, God had already decreed how he would fix our mistakes." He made provision before the foundation of the world so that when we mess up in time, He can restore us back to His eternal plan. So when we mess up we can connect from the present back to the past and realign our future.

TRANSITIONS OF TIME

A transition is a passage from one state, stage, subject, or place to another. Transitions occur because there comes a necessary time for change in a movement, by evolving from one form, stage, or style to another; new developments occur in our life processes. At every transition, we cross over! We are God's children through Jesus Christ; we have been grafted into the new covenant through his blood. Therefore, we are a people who are always crossing over. We are always changing! In order to move across and occupy our inheritance we must come to an ending or death of one phase of our life. We must let go of one thing to embrace something new. We are a people who do not like to die, we resist change! Therefore, we usually hang on with all of our strength to something in a phase of our life that is ending instead of gracefully releasing one good thing for something better. Let me explain: As a young man growing up in the Bronx, NY, I had but one goal, to make it to the Major Leagues in Baseball. I stayed away from drugs, alcohol, women, parties everything. Why? Because I was perfecting the game of baseball so I could become who I wanted to be, A Major League Baseball player! Hundreds of hours playing and perfecting the game, catching ground balls, hitting a baseball. Suddenly, I get saved and God wants me to quit the game. I resisted this call. I could not allow my mind to embrace this new way, this new revelation. I was not clear exactly how to advance or cross over to something new. I was perplexed, confused, and frustrated so I resisted the transition. However, in my refusal to cross over there was sadness and pain. The pain of leaving something I dearly loved for something I knew nothing about. I decided to do it after two years of resisting it, this was the pain phase of change. See, leaving behind the old can be painful, and at times we have to face pain to advance. In every process we must remember that the best is yet ahead and that the process of transition we are in will produce a new beginning.

THIS IS THE OPPORTUNE TIME OF YOUR LIFE

The word Chronos refers to the general process of time or chronological time. The word Kairos refers to the right time, the opportune or strategic time, the now time. So Kairos, in many ways, is an extension or continuation of Chronos. As the processes of God's plan unfold, Chronos becomes Kairos. The new is connected to the old and in fact, is often the result of what happened in the old. My Kairos moments were when I was a child, when I was in my early 20's and when I was 32.

HEARING GODS VOICE

I heard a voice inside of me say JUMP! when I was just ten years old and it saved me from a terrible injury in Havana, Cuba where I was born. I was in a little wooden wheel car that my brother and I built. We were going down a steep hill near our home and then I heard the word JUMP! So, I did! My brother who was driving and his friend both failed to make the turn at the bottom of the hill and sure enough, it hit a parked car, and both were badly injured. However, I only had some minor scratches. I did not know then what I know now that God can speak to you in that way at any time. On another occasion, I was in Key west, Florida going over the seven-mile bridge with the intentions of taking my life. I was frustrated because my first girlfriend who I was engaged to be married left me for another. At hearing the news, I took the 1967 Galaxy 500 I had just bought at a fair price and headed to the bridge going 120mph. I did not care where my car was going to land or what would happen to me. As I approached the 120mph I heard a voice say "Look to the left" so I looked and saw a vast body of water. Again, the voice said "look to the right" so I looked again all I saw was a vast body of water. Then the voice spoke again and said, "There are plenty of fish in the ocean." It was a statement, a saying I had learned in High School which meant there is more than one woman out there to pick from. With that understanding I immediately stopped the car and did not kill myself. See God will speak to us in our own language, he will use our own way of understanding to keep us from harming ourselves. That is why is so important to quiet our lives and focus on the inner voice that we have which is what God calls in the Bible His still small voice. "Be still and know that I am God." (Psalm 46:10)

At the homeless shelter, in Clinton, Iowa, where I am the executive director, we have a one hour soaking every Friday morning where all the men get to meditate on spiritual songs and I teach them to concentrate and pay attention to the lyrics of these songs to help them hear from God as they quiet their spirits. Soaking basically means being saturated in God's presence. When we do that, we can learn to hear God's inner voice. Prayer is not a monologue it is a dialogue between you and the Lord. God wants you to speak but he too wants to speak to us.

It was 1981, I was in Clinton, Iowa and the spirit of

the Lord was prompting me to begin a church work. I was undecided because of all my obligations to family and work. But one day I am taking a shower and I hear the words, "THE MOMENT IS RIGHT NOW." I proceeded to put my bathrobe on and I headed to my bedroom. To my surprise, I saw a red button in the middle of my bed with yellow letters. It said, "THE MOMENT IS RIGHT NOW." I began to weep bitterly, not believing what I had just experienced. I ran out of the room to tell my wife what had just happened. When I came back to my bedroom to show her the button the button disappeared. I am sure the initial reaction of my wife then was unbelief. But the bible says angels are the messengers of God and he will send them with specific orders to bring us to His divine purposes.

WE ARE PEOPLE ON THE MOVE

Human beings as a general rule are people always on the move. We are moving our residences from one place to another. We are moving from one work position to another. We change vocations in life. Life has many passages that we must face with faith and courage. I was glad that although I resisted the change to go from a baseball player into a preacher that my decision to go through this phase magnificently transformed my life to great victory. I could venture to say that every transition in life is different and entails a different set of circumstances and events. Therefore, each transition has a time element and a narrow place that we need to navigate through. We must remember that we all go through transitions, but you must end one and begin another to keep moving into your next place or else you will remain miserably in your present transition, and it will become your future. So, make a decision today to cross over because time is running out from us. Your time upon this earth is in God's hand and the Kingdom of God is advancing and it needs you to transition from the old to the new. In 2 Corinthians 5:17 it says, "Therefore, if anyone is in Christ, he is a new creation; the old has gone, the new has come!"

RAY GIMENEZ AND LYLE WILKINS PRAYING

VICTORY CENTER'S WORK

CHAPTER 4

POSITIONING YOURSELF AWAY FROM SICKNESS: THE REAL MEANING OF SICKNESS

In 1977, I was working as a meter reader in Con Edison in Bronx, New York. I knocked on the door to gain access into a house to read the meters and I meet a crying mother. I asked what was the matter? She promptly replied, "my only daughter has terminal cancer." I explained I am a Christian and that I knew Jesus can heal her. I asked for her name and she replied that she would be leaving her 3 young children behind to my amazement her dying daughter was sent home to die. She was laying on the sofa in the living room. I proceeded to introduce myself and I asked her if I could pray for her. She said yes. After prayer, I told her that nothing is impossible with God, that I expected her to be healed. She was 35 years old at the time. When I came back a month later to read the meters, again mom greeted me at the door only to tell me that her daughter was healed, and the cancer was gone! Wow! I was not a Pastor at the time just a young man on fire for God. But this healing revolutionized my life. This family invited me to have lunch with them which I did, and I realized then that God wants to take care of his children. This event, this healing, marked my life forever, it was the first time I had done something like this. God does not bring sickness, but he provides us with power and opportunities to heal others in His name. We are not merely a bunch of dirt thrown together to exist for a few decades and then die. We're built for God's purposes to see God's Kingdom advance through ruling over darkness. Sickness is always darkness. In San Francisco I placed my finger in an ear of a man who was a Mexican, he was deaf in that ear for 10 years and God immediately healed him while he was driving. He became a good song writer and guitar player for Jesus after that. On another occasion in Costa Rica, I prayed for a 3-year-old boy born blind and he was healed in just 10 minutes. In the many countries that I have traveled I have seen chronic back pain ailments healed, legs growing, arthritis disappearing, migraines and fevers annihilated all through the power of prayer. Jesus said that if you believe in Him signs, wonders, and miracles will happen. He puts it this way in Mark 16:17-18, "and these signs will accompany those who believe in my name they will drive out demons; they will speak in new tongues; they will pick up snakes with their hands and when they drink deadly poison and it will not hurt them at all. They will place their hands-on sick people and they will get well." Let us now look deeper into the real meaning of sickness.

Because of my many healings that I have experienced in my own life, and the many more I have witnessed myself in the United States and abroad I would like to spend some time now in the next few pages talking about how to have victory over sickness. First let me just add right here that in my studies of the Bible I have concluded that 2/3 of Christ life in ministry was spent healing people. Either he was coming from healing someone, on the way to healing someone, or actually engaged in healing someone. It was his passion and desire to make people well. So, in the next few pages let's look at this word sickness and understand its roots.

IN GOD'S ORIGINAL CREATION THERE IS NO SICKNESS

Let's look at reasons we are sure it is God's will to heal. You may find that you have heard some of these things before but read them like you have never heard them. If some people ate their physical food like they hear the Word of God, they would have starved to death a long time ago. It would be like taking a tray to the cafeteria, setting things on it, and saying, "Oh, salad- I had that in 1972. Oh, beans-I had them in 1965."

If you're not going to eat the same things you've eaten before, you're going to starve. Jesus said,

"Man shall not live by bread alone, but by every Word that proceeds out of the mouth of God." (Matthew 4:4)

Do you know why you're supposed to hear the same word again? It feeds your spirit, and as you grow, you get more out of it than you did the last time. As you grow and develop, you see things you didn't see in a verse before.

So read these things like you haven't heard them, because in truth, there are things here we've not seen before. If you have heard them before, you still need to be fed on them. You need to feed your spirit. It feeds you even more than you realize, because there are things on a level that's above and beyond your conscience.

Genesis One is the beginning of what we know. The Bible says in Genesis 1:3-4, "And God said, let there be light: and there was light. And God saw the light, that it was good.

> *Verse 10 says, "And God called the dry land Earth; and the gathering together of the waters called the Seas: and God saw that it was good."*

> *Verse 18 says, "And He gave these lights to rule over the day and over the night, and to divide the light from darkness: and God saw it was good."*

Verse 21 says, "And God created great whales, and every living creature that moveth, which the waters brought forth abundantly, after their kind, and every winged fowl after his kind, and God saw it was good."

Are you seeing a recurring theme here? God made something, and what? It was good. He made something else, and it was good. Then he made more things, and they were good.

Verse 25 says, "And God made the beast of the Earth after his kind, and cattle after their kind, and everything that creepth upon the earth after his kind: and God saw that it was good."

God made man, and then verse 28 says, "And God blessed them, and God said unto them, be fruitful and multiply, and replenish the earth, and subdue it: and have dominion over (it)." Verse 29 says, "And God said, Behold, I have given you (seed)... "and it verse 31 it says, " And God saw everything that he had made, and behold, it was very good. And the evening and the morning were the sixth day."

If you look up the word translated "very," it is the word "mighty." So, I guess we're accurate in the southern United

States when we say, "That was mighty good." We're correct with the original Hebrew language. "Mighty meaning "powerful good," which is another way of saying "very." Very is great, but I like "mighty." It might even be more accurate. "Mighty good!"

God saw everything that He made, and it was mighty good. How about God? God is mighty. He's powerfully good, He is mighty good, and everything He made was good. When did He make the bad things? When did God create cancer? On the first day? On the third day? When did God create Aids? On what day? What part of creation? When did that come into being during His creation? First, second, third, fourth, fifth, sixth day? On what day did He create arthritis? He didn't. Sickness and disease are not part of God's original creation. You can't look at cancer and say, "Behold, it is very good." You can't look at Aids, abscesses, and growths as mighty good." No. They are not good. Sickness is not good.

I know this sounds simplistic, but there are still millions of Christians who will tell you, "Well maybe God had some kind of purpose in it. I know it's an awful thing, but really, I think maybe it was a blessing in disguise."

It's either good or it's bad, and God does not confuse us. Everything that God made was mighty fine and mighty good. Everything was good, including Adam and Eve. Do you believe Adam was "defect-free"? Eve was "deformity-free"? They had no flaws or deformities.

They had no disease in them at all. They were brilliant. They were magnificent, weren't they? Their bodies were perfect, and their minds were amazing and perfect. They talked with God in the afternoon about things He wanted to talk about, and they understood them.

I'm sorry, but I don't accept the version of them sitting in a cave naked going, "Ugh. Ugh. Ugh." I don't believe it. There may be some people who fell to near animalistic states centuries after creation, but no, Adam and Eve were brilliant and perfect. In their brilliant state, if you would have told them," I have a headache," they would have looked at you puzzled and said,"

"A what? What is that?"

"My head hurts. It's pounding. A headache!"

They'd look at you like... "What?" They had nothing with which to reference it. Nothing. They didn't know what it was like to have an "off' day "I just feel a little off today. I don't know... I'm a little bit slow, a little bit weak."

They wouldn't even understand what you were talking about, because when God made them, He made them perfect, whole, and strong. If disease pleased the Father, He would have made them with diseases. If deformities and sickness was His will, He would have created Adam and Eve with them built right in from the start. Anything that came along later, because of sin, death, and curse, is not an improvement on God's original creation, and it is not good.

God hates sickness. That's a big statement, but I want you to think about it now. He hates sin, and death is His enemy. You hear some preachers standing over caskets talking about how God took this one in death and healed them through death because He loved them and wanted them to be with Him more than anyone else. They say that talking about a 20-year-old who died in car a crash.

Death is the enemy of God. I Corinthians 15:26-27 says that, "death is the last enemy that shall be put under foot." It was not part of His original creation. When God created everything, nothing died. Nothing. Flowers didn't die. Trees didn't die. Animals didn't die, and men and women did not die.

We need to be reminded of this. Everything that you and I have known since we came into this world is warped. It's twisted. It's distorted form the way God made it. Even in its fallen condition, this planet is amazing, but we need to remind ourselves that it's messed up. The Bible says that it is groaning and travailing. (Romans 8:22) Why? It's dying. The planet is dying just like we are. It's been cursed. That's why the plates are shifting, causing volcanic eruptions and hurricanes. This is not the will of God. This is not what God created; it's been messed up. It's off. Why? Sin messed it all up.

Oh, but He's going to fix it. He already has the plan in operation. It's just a matter of time.

What we need to know right here and now in this life,

is what is good and what is evil, what is of God and what is not of God. We need to know what we are to receive and bear patiently, and what we are to resist with everything that is in us. Christians have been lied to because they've been told from pulpits that God is teaching them something through sickness. God sent it on them to develop some kind of piety or some kind of spirituality, and they're supposed to bear it with meekness and patience. It's a lie. Sickness is evil. I'm going to prove it to you, if you'll receive scriptures.

MY HEALINGS

His healing power over me initiated God's mission for my life and ministry. In 1986 working for 3M in Cordova, Illinois, I hurt my back while trying to pick up a 400 pound tote tank it was really my ignorance, I just did not want to look bad in front of my supervisors since the tote tank fell off my pallet as I was driving a fork truck. At the hospital the next day in Clinton, Iowa, they were talking surgery for my lower back. Here I was stretched out in a bed in tractions. That means ropes all around me. I looked like an octopus! At about three in the morning I began reading my bible and came across the scripture in Matthew were God was saying when I was hungry you gave me something to eat, when I was thirsty you gave me something to drink, when I was naked you clothed me. Suddenly these scriptures jumped out of their pages and I felt the Lord saying, "Start a Mission for the homeless." I immediately began to argue with the Lord, I started telling him that I was working full time forty to 50 hours a week, I was pastoring a church, and I had six kids to take care of with my wife. God persisted in giving me this assignment so then I asked him "if you heal me right now, I will do this for you." So, in an instant the Lord said, "get out of traction." I did this but it took me an hour to try to unravel myself without any pain whatsoever then I knew I was instantly healed. I knew now I had to fulfill the assignment he had asked me to start, a Mission for the homeless. I put my clothes on by myself, got my bag and walked out to the nurse's station. The nurses were extremely mad when they saw me, I insisted in telling them that I had a godly visitation and that God had healed me. But they insisted even harder and advised me to see the doctor in the morning and let him decide whether to release me or not. I obeyed! But what I didn't like is that they placed me back in tractions. Back to being like an octopus!

The doctor came in the morning as planned he had heard the good and bad news of what had happened. He proceeded to take the octopus clothes off of me then he said, "Stand up." Gee, where did I hear that before? Then he said, "touch your toes but don't bend your knees." So, I did again without any pain. He urged me to do it again, and again and again. When he noticed I had no pain he was in unbelief. With an angry countenance, he took me into the x-ray room. A time later he discovered I had no back injury that would require surgery, so he decided to write a document to my employer to give me three months off for intense therapy three to four times a week. I knew I did not need the therapy and I told him so, but he was taking every precaution. Those three months with full compensation by my employer were used to begin planning the work for the

Lord. God will always create the situation for his perfect healing to get his purposes done for his kingdom.

HIS WILL FOR HEAVEN AND THE WORLD TO COME

John saw into the future by the Spirit of God. He saw what's still ahead of us. This is not a fairy tale or just something that someone imagined. This is your future that we're reading about right here. In a very short time, you and I and many more like us will be experiencing these verses. Can you get excited about it? This is our future.

In Revelations 21:1, He said, "And I saw a new heaven and a new earth: for the first heaven and first earth were passed away..." What happened to the old earth? It passed away.

Some say, "Save the planet!" We can't save it. Now, there's no need in seeing how quickly we can mess it up, but we are not going to save the planet. Revelation even tells us how it's going to end. I won't get into that, but it describes it exactly, talking about things that scientists have talked about. It already tells us how it's happening. The planet is not going to survive like it is. How is it going to end? The Bible says the elements are going to melt with fervent heat. The whole surface of the planet is going to melt. The surface, the atmosphere, everything is going. The planet as we know it is going to be gone. (2 Peter 3:10)

But God is creating a new one that is perfect, the way

He started the old one, and you and I are going to be there and be part of it. This time, nobody is messing it up.

You might ask me, "Do you really believe all that?" Every word and it makes me happy, too. John said, "And I saw a new heaven and a new earth: for the first heaven and the first earth were passed away; and there was no more sea." You've got a lot more real estate like that, because most of the planet is covered in water. He said in verse 2, "I saw the holy city, new Jerusalem coming down from God out of heaven, prepared as a bride adorned for her husband." God's going to live with us. Hallelujah! Verse 3 says, "I heard a great voice out of heaven saying, Behold, the tabernacle of God is with men, and he will dwell with them, and they shall be his people, and God himself shall be with them, and be their God."

Someone might ask, "Where do you stay? Where do you live?"

"I live with God. We all live in the same place. We live with Him. He lives with us." Glory to God!

They will ask, "Where is God?"

You will say, "He's right over there? Do you want to go see Him?"

We'll be able to physically- in bodies that you can touch-walk to the throne. We will live together. It makes you want to say, "Come quickly, Lord Jesus, let's do it now." It will happen quickly enough.

Why is He tarring? There are a lot of people who don't know Him yet. A lot of people need to be saved. It's His mercy that He is tarrying.

In verse 4, what does it say is going to happen? "And God shall wipe away all tears from their eyes; and there shall be no more death..." Paradise is regained. Paradise is restored. The original creation, the original and perfect plan and will of God, is restored-back to the way He intended it before it got messed up. No more death.

"Neither sorrow," which means no more grief, no more depression, "nor crying." What about that? No more sobbing. What else? "Neither shall there be any more pain..." Now pain covers everything from stubbing your toe to a toothache to a terminal disease. No more pain. None!

"for the former things are passed away."

It would be difficult to find a Christian who has been around church at all, or read a Bible, who wouldn't quickly agree with you and say, "Yes, that is how it will be in heaven."

"How many sick people are there in heaven?" "None, there are no sick people."

How many blind people, deaf people, and deformed people?" "None. There are no sick people up there. None are sick."

GOD'S WILL

So, we're in agreement that it is not God's will for any

sickness, disease, or death in heaven or in the world to come. But what about the question, "Is it His will, though, for people to be sick and suffering on the earth?" Millions would say, "Well, obviously, sometimes it is." So, you're saying that God has a different will for the earth than He does for heaven?

Does God really have two different wills for heaven and earth? Lots of people learn about this in Sunday school, in Matthew 6. People call it "The Lord's Prayer."

He said in Matthew 6:9-10, "After this manner pray: Our Father which art in heaven, Hallowed be they name. Thy kingdom come, Thy will be done in earth, as it is in heaven."

How are we to understand this? Millions of people believe that God has a purpose for people being sick and suffering on the earth, although they would never agree it might be His will for them to be sick in heaven."

People say, "Well, I want to hurry up and get to heaven, so I don't have to deal with all of this sickness and disease." I thought you said it's God's will for you to be sick.

"I believe it; God put this on me to teach me something or to glorify Himself." Well, don't be in a hurry to get to heaven, then, because in heaven, His will is unhindered and perfected. If it's His will for you to be sick down here, you'll be much sicker in heaven.

They say, "No! No, I won't."

He doesn't change, and His will doesn't change. In

the beginning, in His creation, what was His will? It was wholeness, soundness, life, no death, and no suffering. What is His will when everything is restored? It's the same: wholeness, soundness, strength, no death, no pain, and no dying. What happened in the middle here? Did he change? No, He does not change. His will now is the same as when he made Adam and Eve. It's the same as it's going to be when this earth is gone.

He told us to pray that His will would be done on earth just like it is in heaven. That tells us something: it is not being done in its completion. If it was, why would we need to pray that it would be? There are all kinds of things happening on the earth that are not the will of God and that don't please God. So, we are to pray that His will would be done.

We're sure it's God's will for all to be healed because of God's will in heaven and the world to come.

THE ORIGIN OF SICKNESS

If God didn't create sickness and disease, it is not a part of His original plan, will, or purpose for us. When everything is fixed, it will be gone again.

So how did sickness get here? Where did it come from? Romans 5: 11-12 tells us. He said,

"but we also have joy in God through our Lord Jesus Christ, by whom we have now received the atonement," or other translations say "reconciliation," "wherefore, as by one man sin entered into the world, and death by sin;

and so death passed upon all men, for that all have sinned." How did death get in? Was there death in God's original creation? No. But this is all we've ever known: thorns and briars, viciousness of nature, storms, and aging. That's all we've known since we've been here. People think this is normal, but it is not normal to God.

When everything is restored, Isaiah said, "the lion is going to lie down with the lamb. A little baby is going to play at the snake's den, and nobody is going to get hurt." (Isaiah 1 1:6-8) There will be nothing to step on and get hurt. The animals are not going to kill each other anymore.

You ask, "How will that work?" Carnivores will be vegetarians. The Bible says that the lion will eat straw like an ox. All of this violence of animals tearing each other apart was never meant to be. It's not God's plan and will, and neither is men killing each other. How did this death get in there? Sin. We should not make light of sin. People sometimes just sin and sin, and you try to talk to them about the seriousness of it and the repercussions of it, and they say, "I'll just apply 1 John 1:9, "If we confess our sins, he is faithful and just to forgive us our sins, and to cleanse us from all unrighteousness" to it. What's the big deal?" The big deal is what sin has done to us, and what it took to get sin off of us, the price that had to be paid. Sin is serious.

We should not take sin lightly. We live in a society where the church belittles sin. They don't even want to use the word anymore. People don't have to sin; they just have problems in today's society. They have problems in today's society. They have problems that they're working on, which means "leave me alone, and I'll change if and when I get good and ready." It's a big problem.

Did you know it pays to sin? Romans 6:23 says, "For the wages of sin and death... "What are wages? Wages are "pay."

You ask, "Did I read that right? It pays to sin?"

You read right. It pays to sin. What does it mean? "The wages," the pay, "of sin is death." It pays to sin, but the pay is death.

You say, "Yes, but I'm in the new covenant, and we're under grace today, so I can just sin."

No, you're going to get paid. You cannot just sin and sin and sin. What people don't understand is that crying because you got caught is not repenting. What does repentance mean? "Repent" means "to change." You can cry all night, and if you don't change the next day, you didn't repent; nothing has changed. Since you didn't repent, you're going to keep getting paid, with death.

This is something I think a lot of people don't understand. They want the blessings of God, but they want to do what they want to do. Can you just yield to your flesh, have all kinds of affairs, hurt people left and right, steal, and lie and then live a long time, stay healthy, and prosper in God 's best?

Some say, "God will forgive me." He will, and He loves you, but it will cost you. Even though God loves you and forgives you, you can still disqualify yourself from His best in your life.

Don't battle sin. Sin is serious. Sin is why this world is in a mess, and it irritates me that people blame God. Religious people do it all the time. "Well, we just don't know what God is doing with all of these wars and shortages and famines...

Maybe they're trying to say it in nice tones, but they're saying that God is behind these little children dying from AIDS. They're saying God has some mystical purpose in whole nations of innocent people being wiped out because they're a different religion from someone else. They're saying God has all of this in control, and we don't know why, but He's got some purpose in it. No! No! A thousand times NO! God is a good God. He made everything perfect, and sin messed it up.

Why are all these terrible things happening today? Because man has a free choice, and man has chosen to sin and disobey. But even in the middle of it, you can choose to believe, submit, and obey, and you can be blessed. In the midst of an ugly, mean world, you can be protected. In the midst of a germ ridden, disease filled planet, you can be healed. In the midst of shortage and economic upheaval in the world, you can be prosperous. Yes, you can! You can if you'll obey, listen, and believe.

Where did sickness come from? God didn't create it. It's not part of His plan. Sickness is a part of death. By one man, sin entered in, and death came because of that sin, because the wages of sin is death, (Romans 5:12)

You say, "It doesn't say 'sickness.'" Yes, it does. It also says poverty. It also says every kind of harassment and confusion and any form of death. If you get enough poverty in your life, you're dead. Enough poverty means you don't even have enough food and drink to keep your body alive. If you get enough sickness in your body, you're dead, right? It's just different degrees of death. None of it would be here if it hadn't been sin, and to say that sickness- which is a product of sin- is the will of God, is tantamount to saying that what caused it is the will of God. You might as well say, "Sin is in the will of God." If there had never been any sin, there would never have been any death, sickness, or poverty.

John Alexander Dowie said this: "Sickness is the foul offspring of its father Satan and its mother sin." He said that at the turn of the century. "Sickness is the foul offspring..." and it is foul, "of its father Satan and its mother sin." To say sickness is the will of God is equal to saying sin is the will of God, because sickness is the product of sin. I know that's a strong statement but disprove it.

We're sure it's God's will for all of us to be healed today because if there had never been any sin, there wouldn't have been any sickness or death or any such thing. So, the products of sin cannot be the will of God. Now don't take that and twist it into something that I didn't say. Some would say, "Are you saying I'm sick because I've sinned?"

Well, you have sinned-that's a given. The Bible says. "Death passed upon all men for that all have sinned." (Romans 5: 12) Death is on the planet because sin is here, and whether you have knowingly violated laws or whether you just ignorantly didn't resist death, it is here because of sin. You can't say, "Well, Adam, you and Eve messed this whole thing up for us. You messed it up!" No, you sinned too. Death passed upon all men because all have sinned.

But glory to God, there's been a cure for sin, and if there's been a cure for sin, then why can't you be healed? If sickness is a result of sin, and sin has been taken care of, then why couldn't a man be healed? Well, you can. You've got just as much right to be healed as you do to be forgiven; it's based on the same work of Jesus.

Remember in James 5:14-15 when he said, "Is there any sick among you? Let him call for the elders of the church; and let them pray over him, anointing him with oil in the name of the Lord: And the prayer of faith shall save the sick, and the Lord shall rise him up; and if he hath committed sins, they shall be forgiven him." Forgiven and healed, in the same prayer.

Jesus looked at the person and said, "Rise, take up your bed and walk," after He said, "Your sins are forgiven." Why? He asked, "Which one is easier to say?" They're the same, because the fix for sin is the fix for everything that came as a result of sin. Glory to God.

SICKNESS IS OF THE DEVIL

Job 2:7 says, "So went Satan forth from the presence of the Lord, and smote Job with sore boils from the sole of his foot unto his crown." Who did it? Satan did it.

The New Living Translation says, "Satan left the Lord's presence, and he struck Job with a terrible case of boils from head to foot." Who did it? Satan did it.

Now, just a few verses later, Job says, "The Lord giveth and the Lord taketh away. Blessed be the name of the Lord." It's good that Job didn't turn against the Lord or curse Him, but Job did not know that the devil did this to him. As you read scripture after scripture and chapter after chapter, you see that Job was completely oblivious to the devil.

Job was in the dark about who was doing this to him, but millions of Christians who are still accusing God of making them sick have no excuse. We have the Bible, right? If the Bible says the devil did it, why would you keep saying God is doing it?

The Bible says, "In the mouth of two or three witnesses shall every word be established." (2 Corinthians 13:1) In Job's case, here's one witness: Who does the Bible say made Job sick? It's inescapable. According to Job 2:7, it is clear that the devil did it; he made Job sick.

In Psalm 41:8, what kind of disease is it talking about? Do you know of any scriptures that talk about good diseases? "An evil disease, say they, cleaveth fast unto him: and now that he lieth he shall rise up no more." The International version calls it "a vile disease." Sickness is vile.

I want you to see this verse in the Young's Literal Translation because Young is the same author of Young's Analytical Concordance. If you want a really good literal translation, look at that. It's not easy to read, but it's just like the original. He says, "A thing of Belial is poured out on him." Who is Belial? Belial is a name for the devil, right? "A thing of the devil." What is he talking about? He is talking about disease. So that makes two witnesses.

Did you see that phrase "evil disease"? God is not involved in anything evil, is He? Certainly not. Is disease evil? The psalm says it is. Is sickness evil? You'll hear people saying, "Well, we just don't really know what's good and what's evil. God knows, and we don't know enough to know. I mean, maybe we think this disease is bad, but you know, it may be good, and we just don't know it." Have you ever heard people talking like this? Are we really to believe that God does not want us to know the difference between what's good and what's evil? Then how would we know if we have His will or we don't, or whether we are doing His will or not?

If someone asks, "Are you doing good?" Do you answer, "I don't know, I'm doing evil, but it might be good, because you just never know"?

Or, "This thing on your life- is it bad or good?" Do you say, "I don't know, God is so high above us and beyond us, we just can't understand His ways, and I know it feels bad, and I don't like it, but it could be good."

Then you are hopelessly confused as to whether you're in the will of God or out of the will of God, or whether you should receive something or resist it.

People say, "I feel confused, but that's just the way it is."

No, that is not the way it is. Ephesians tells us not to be foolish or unwise, but to understand what the will of the Lord is. (5:17) that's why He gave us the Bible. That's why He gave us the Holy Spirit. He's not trying to hide things from us. He wants us to know plainly and clearly. If it's good, receive it. If it's evil, resist it. If it's good, do it. If it's evil, stay away from it. He wants us to be crystal clear on what's good and what's evil. Leaving baseball, leaving 3M.

Well, what do you need to convince you that sickness is bad? We have two witnesses already. What's a witness in Job? The devil did it. Who made Job sick? The devil did it, as plain as you can read it.

The psalm says that disease is a thing of the devil, and it's evil.

There are some more witnesses in the New Testament. In Luke 13, a woman was bent over for 18 years and couldn't straighten herself up. Jesus spoke to her that she was loosed. He laid His hands on her, and immediately she straightened up and glorified God. Nothing is said about her glorifying God those 18 years that she was stooped over. But as soon as she was loosed and straightened up, it says that she glorified God.

In verse 14, it says, "And the ruler of the synagogue answered with indignation, because Jesus had healed on the Sabbath day, and said unto the people, there are six days in which men ought to work: in them therefore come and be healed, and not on the Sabbath day." Hypocrite! They never had a healing day. They never had a day when they were going to lay hands on her, the Lord then answered him and said, "Thou hypocrite...." "You hypocrites." When Jesus calls you a hypocrite, you're a hypocrite. "Thou hypocrite, doth not each one of you on the Sabbath lose his ox or his ass from the stall, and lead him away to watering? And ought not this woman, being a daughter of Abraham, whom Satan hath bound these eighteen years, be loosed from this bond on the Sabbath day?"

What was wrong with her? She was physically bent over. You've seen folks like that, who couldn't straighten up. She was bent over. People might have called it "curvature of the spine," or just arthritis. It was some kind of disease that had her bent over, and what did Jesus say it was? That it was His Father teaching her something? No. Where did this come from then? Who did that to this woman?

Some might say, "Well, now, it said in that specific instance that the devil did it. But sometimes it's the Lord working it out... Sometimes it's the devil, and sometimes it's the Lord, and you just never know what God's going to. . . "Do you see how ignorant this is? Do God and the devil ever swap jobs? There are people who will try to tell you that sometimes the devil heals people, and there are a lot of people who will tell you that God makes people sick for numerous and varied reasons. They are just completely ignoring verse after verse of Scripture.

Here's a third witness. It ought to be established by now, in the mouths of two or three witnesses. Job 2:7 says that the devil made him sick. Psalm 41 says that sickness is an evil thing, a thing of the devil. In Luke 13:16, Jesus, the Head of the Church, who knows what He's talking about, calls this woman's physical problem "satanic bondage." Doesn't he? I accept that.

Say this out loud: "Sickness is of the devil. It's evil, satanic bondage." We're quoting the Bible.

We are sure, convinced, and persuaded that it's God's will-His perfect will-for all of us to be healed today. Why? Among other reasons, because sickness is a work of the devil.

How about another witness? Acts 10:38 says, "How God anointed Jesus of Nazareth with the Holy Ghost and with power: who went about doing good... "Did He ever do any evil? Of course not. He only did good, and what was part of good He was doing? "He went about doing good and healing all that were oppressed of the devil; for God was with Him." According to the Holy Spirit, speaking here through the Book of Acts, everyone to whom Jesus ministered healing was oppressed of God, or that God put sickness on them to teach them something. No, everyone who Jesus healed, the Scripture says, was satanically oppressed. According to Acts 10:38, sickness and disease are satanic oppression.

We could keep going, but are four witnesses enough? How many more do we need? In the mouths of two, it can be established from the Bible.

Let's go over these again. Job 2:7 says that the devil made me sick. It doesn't say God did it. The devil did it. Psalm 41 says that disease is evil, a thing of Belial, a thing of the devil. Luke 13: 16 says that sickness is satanic bondage, and to the woman who was bound, Jesus said, "She ought to be free. She ought to be loosed from the satanic bondage."

You never hear Him saying God was teaching her something, or that it wasn't God's timing for her to be healed yet. You hear that out of the mouths of preachers, or in seminaries, but you never hear it in the New Testament.

Jesus ministered to a lot of people. The Bible says that multitudes were healed in one day, multitudes being thousands. Matthew 12:15, and 19:2, It says "that as many as had this or that wrong with them, when they brought them to Jesus, again and again they were healed-every one of them; they were all healed." Not even one was told, "It's not time. Sorry, not for you. No, not yet." No, all were healed. It says all of them that were healed- and there were many, all oppressed of the devil. The devil did it. It was a thing of the devil, satanic bondage, and satanic oppression. Is that enough for us to believe that sickness is bad and that it is a work of the devil?

Could God want "a work of the devil" in us? Could it please Him? A work of Belial? An evil thing to be working in us.

I'm telling you; God hates disease. Now, don't feel bad if you've got some symptoms or problems in your body; don't go that direction with it. You just need to know what to resist and what to receive, and you must be crystal clear that God's not wanting you to yield to this or have this. This is not something that's pleasing Him on any level. When God made man, He made man spectacular. He made Adam and Eve beautiful and glorious. But disease has taken this beautiful creation and twisted it, deformed it, and messed it up until at times, I've seen disease put such a force on a body that it didn't even look human. How could God be pleased with something that messed up his perfect creation like that? No way. It displeases Him. It is not His will.

What does that mean? It means you have every right to stand against it. You have every right to resist it, and to say, "No, I don't have to yield to this because it is no the will of God for me."

Say this out Loud:

> *Sickness is not the will of God for me. Disease will never be God's will for me. It cannot be. Healing is His will for me*

CHAPTER 5

DEVELOPING YOUR JOY FOR THE LORD

The Bible says in Nehemiah 8:10, "Don't be dejected and sad, for the joy of the Lord is your strength!" It doesn't say exercise your strength, or hard work is your strength, or winning the lottery is your strength. It doesn't even say joy is your strength. It's the joy that comes from the Lord that is our strength.

Some of us are weary, and we think maybe it's because we're overworked or not getting enough sleep. So, we take sleeping pills and buy mattresses intelligent enough to have a measurable IQ, and we try to get some rest. And yet, we still feel lethargic. Our strength seems zapped.

The problem isn't a lack of sleep; it's a lack of joy. Our strength is connected to our joy, and our joy is connected to the gospel we believe in.

I'm not promoting fake joy, the smile-for-the-camera kind of joy that doesn't make it past your Botox. It's not about forcing laughter and bubbly words just so you'll look spiritual.

"Well, I read this book that says I have to be joyful. Because, you know, joy is part of the gospel. And I want to look like someone who believes the gospel, and if I don't smile a lot, it makes God look bad." So, we laugh and smile and high-five everyone, but at home we're grouchier than ogres with hemorrhoids.

The joy of the Lord is authentic. It seeps into the core of who we are and holds us in perpetual state of peace and happiness. The joy of the Lord strengthens us, soothes us and sustains us.

True happiness is a state of being, not just passing emotion. Even when external circumstances rock our emotions for a time, we are able to strengthen ourselves by trusting in the Lord.

David prayed this prayer, recorded in Psalm 51: 12 "Restore to me the joy of your salvation." A lot of times it gets misquoted as "Restore to me the joy of my salvation." It's not my salvation-it's God's. I am not the originator or the creator. It's His work of grace. It's His initiative.

There is a perpetual state of joy that comes with the gospel. No matter what we are going through, no matter what circumstances we are facing right now, when we understand the gospel, it will keep us in a state of happiness and joy.

It's God's grace, God's joy and God's strength- and we have free and complete access to it. It doesn't get better than that. KEEP YOUR JOY.

CREATING YOUR DAILY SUCCESS ROUTINE - HERE'S A GOOD LIST

1. **Recognize what is worthy of your total focus today.** Everyone will have a different focus. Target what you desire the most.

2. **Pinpoint the top three distractions that occur habitually.** Leaders fail because of broken focus. Satan cannot destroy you, merely distract you.

3. **Pray continuously in the Holy Spirit.** He has an agenda. You must discern His agenda and not decide on your own.

4. **Determine the core product of your life.** What do you want to do the most? What is the legacy you desire to leave? Everything does not have equal value. Everyone does not deserve equal time.

5. **Embrace flexibility as an opportunity.** "I've never had a plan yet where everything happened as I planned it." Take advantage of the unexpected.

6. **Here's my last statement.** "Nothing bothers me." Everything is subject to change."

7. **Recognize those around you who do not have a determined focus or goal.** They want your attention and they do not hesitate to break your focus.

8. **Keep a visual picture of your desired goal and dream before you.** Abraham had a picture of the stars and the sand of the sea a personal motivation for His generations of children. Joseph had a picture of Himself in authority. Jesus had a picture of returning to his Father.

9. **Become militant about keeping your daily success routine.** One of the happiest seasons of my life was 13 years ago. I birthed a daily success routine. I went to bed at 10:30 P.M. I arose at 5:00 A.M. And read by Bible for 20 minutes, then prayed for 40 minutes. Then went in my spa for 12 minutes, into my exercise room for 25 minutes and into the shower room. My joy was remarkable. My peace was unexplainable. When I do not do this my entire rhythm is affected. Something is lost that I cannot explain. A good habit is too powerful to treat lightly. Become militant about keeping it.

KEEP YOUR JOY BY CREATING YOUR DREAM WALL

Decide what you really want. Jesus knew His purpose and mission. "For the Son of man is come to seek and to save that which was lost." (Luke 19: 10).

At age 13, I made the decision to be a professional baseball player. At age 27 I made the decision to be a minister. Write down your 12 goals you want to accomplish this year. Remember your goals will change throughout your life. Things so vital to you at 20 years of age will become unimportant to you at thirty. Here's some helpful hints:

1. Invest one hour in writing down clearly the goals that really matter to you. "Write the vision, and make it plain upon tables, that He may run that readeth it," (Habakkuk 2:2)

2. Permit unexciting dreams of yesterday to die. Stop pursuing something that does not have the ability to excite you anymore. Do not feel obligated to keep trying to obtain it... if you are in a different place in your life.

3. Do not depend on others to understand your dreams and goals. Refuse to be intimidated by their efforts to persuade you to move in a different direction with your life.

4. Never make permanent decisions because of temporary feelings. One young man got so excited about a new friend that he dropped the lease on his own apartment to move in with his friend. Within a week, he realized it was a mistake!

5. Avoid intimate relationships with those who do not really respect your dreams. You will have to sever ties. Wrong people do not always leave your life

voluntarily. Life is too short to permit discourages close to you. "And have no fellowship with the unfruitful works of darkness, but rather reprove them," (Eph. 5:11).

6. Anticipate changes in your goals. Your present feelings and opinions are not permanent. New experiences are coming. New relationships are ahead. STAY CONSCIOUS OF THIS. CREATE YOUR DREAM WALL AND UPDATE CONTINUOUSLY, IT WILL KEEP YOU IN THE JOY OF HIS SPIRIT.

KEEP YOUR JOY BY BECOMING A MASTER PROBLEM SOLVER

You are here for a reason. (Psalm 4:3) "But know that the Lord hath set apart the Godly for Himself. The Bible, the "Manufacturer's Handbook," is filled with examples of those who discovered and embraced their assignment. Moses solved problems for the Israelites. Aaron solved problems for Moses. Jonathan was assigned to David. Jonah was assigned to the Ninevites. A handmaiden helped Naaman get healed. Ruth was assigned to Naomi. We are assigned to solve problems for somebody somewhere.

- You are healer for someone sick and brokenhearted
- You are the life jacket for someone drowning.
- You are the ruler over someone unruly.
- You are the lifter for someone fallen.
- Why am I here? Why me? What is your purpose?

VICTORY CENTER MINISTRIES

GREAT THANKSGIVING BANQUET FOR THE POOR CLINTON IOWA

Your function is different from others. Leaders, counselors or just Christians provide answers to problems.

10 FACTS FOR A MASTER PROBLEM SOLVER

1. Problems are the gates to your significance.
2. Problems are wonderful, glorious seeds for change.

3. Problems will link you to others.
4. Problems provide your income.
5. Problems birth opportunity to reveal your uniqueness.
6. Problems birth new relationships.
7. Problems are the real reason friendships exist.
8. Remove problems from the Earth, and you will destroy any sense of significance in Humanity.
9. Problems bring good people together during bad times.
10. Problems if handled well will build your joy in Him.

REMEMBER THIS

The mechanic knows that an automobile problem is his connection to you. The dentist knows that a tooth problem is his connection to you. The poor and homeless know that the Rescue Mission Leader's problem is connected to you. THE PROBLEM GOD CREATED YOU TO SOLVE ON EARTH IS CALLED YOUR ASSIGNMENT. Become a Master Problem Solver! Keep your Joy.

DON'T WAIT UNTIL IT'S TOO LATE TO FIND REST

YOU CANNOT KEEP YOUR JOY WITHOUT PROPER REST

Looking at a massive to-do list with every item checked off can give us a real boost. If you're like me, we all like knowing we've accomplished many tasks throughout the day. We thrive on getting things done and being productive.

But... is it always healthy? Here's what I've learned. The Bible doesn't command us to live and die by our to-do lists; God doesn't look at our productivity to decide if we're fit for Heaven. When Jesus visited Martha and Mary, He gently scolded Martha for her busyness. Telling her that her sister Mary made the better choice by simply sitting at His feet. (Luke 10:41-42) Jesus didn't praise Martha for being busy; He used her resting sister, Mary, as an example of what was right. You may not accomplish everything you set out to do today. But if you intentionally choose to spend time with the Lord you are following the example of Mary and you will have "chosen what is better."

After coordinating an international conference for my ministry, I was physically exhausted. I had entertained numerous Pastor's, Apostles, and leaders in a two-week span. Right after this I was scheduled to do many other important things. Sometimes the enemy wants us to be buried in busyness like Martha, so we're so buried with stuff that we really are buried. I decided instead to cancel agendas and head out on a 10-hour drive to Tawas Bay, Michigan to rest and reflect. My wife and I her mother, Yvonne, and family members enjoyed the beautiful scenery. The birds, the ducks, the sunrises and sunsets. We enjoyed the gorgeous lake and the fellowship of our family. I came back home well rested and ready to tackle the ministry of reconciliation that the Lord had given me. I've seen so many ministers and leaders burned out because they were like Martha and not Mary. They thought "well if I don't get it done no one will" or "I will be disqualified by Jesus if I don't get it done." Well here's the good news. Jesus said, "I will build my Church." Not us...we're to build disciples. He will take care of His church... God has ordered rest for His sons and daughters...even He God after the 6th day of His creation He took the seventh day and declared it a rest day...A day to reflect on Him. I saw God at Tawas Bay, Michigan. His created animals, birds, water and people... So, stop and smell the roses and don't wait until it's too late. Your joy will increase with rest.

CHAPTER 6

HOW TO RECEIVE JESUS A SAVIOR & BEGIN A NEW LIFE

Step 1 - God loves you and has a plan for you! The Bible says, "God so loved the world that He gave his one and only son, (Jesus Christ), that whoever believes in him shall not perish, but have eternal life." (John 3:16) Jesus said, "I came that they may have life and have it abundantly. "A complete life full of purpose (John 10:10) but here's the problem:

Step 2 - Man is sinful and separated from God. We have all done, thought or said bad things, which the Bible calls sin. "The Bible says." All have sinned and fall short of the Glory of God." (Romans 3:23)

The result of sin is death, spiritual separation from God (Romans 6:23).

The good news?

Step 3 - God sent his son to die for your sins! Jesus died in our place so we could have a relationship with God and be with Him forever.

> *"God demonstrates His own love toward us, in that while we were yet sinners, Christ died for us" (Romans 5:8)*

But it didn't end with His death on the cross. He rose again and still lives!

"Christ died for our sins...He was buried...He was raised on the third day, according to the scriptures" (1 Corinthians 15:3-4) Jesus is the only way to God. Jesus said, "I am the way, and the truth, and the life; no one comes to the father, but through me" (John 14:6)

Step 4 - Would you like to receive God's forgiveness? We can't earn salvation; we are saved by God's grace when we have faith in His son, Jesus Christ. All you have to do is believe you are a sinner that Christ died for your sins and ask forgiveness. Then turn from your sins-that's called repentance. Jesus Christ knows you and loves you. What matters to Him is the attitude of your heart, your honesty and sincerity. I suggest praying the following. Prayer to accept Christ as your Savior and be Born Again!

"Dear God, I know I'm a sinner, and I ask for your forgiveness. I believe Jesus Christ is your son. I believe that he died for my sin and that you raised him to life. I want to trust Him as my Savior and follow Him as Lord. From this day forward. Guide my life and help me to do your will. I pray this in the name of Jesus. Amen."

BORN AGAIN: WELCOME TO THE FAMILY

Congratulations! By receiving Jesus Christ as your Savior, you have begun the most exciting adventure of your life. The purpose of this writing is to help you begin that adventure in Christ on solid footing. So, settle into your chair, ask God to help you understand the words you are about to read, and then let the words and the scriptures written here help you start the exciting journey of your new life.

What exactly has happened to you? Put simply, you have become a child of God, a part of God's spiritual family who receive eternal life with Him in Heaven.

But how did all that happen? First of all, the Bible tells us that all men, because of sin, are separated from God, who is holy and righteous. The Apostle Paul wrote, "All have sinned and fall short of the glory of God" (Romans 3:23). Therefore man, having sinned is cut off from God having no hope of eternal life.

But God, in His great mercy and love, sent His only Son, Jesus Christ, into the world that man might be saved from his sins through Jesus. The Apostle John tells us, "For God so loved the world he gave his only Son, that whoever believes in him should not perish but have eternal life. (John 3:16)

It is through Jesus death on the cross, by shedding of His blood, that you have been redeemed from your sins (see Matthew 26:28, Ephesians 1: 7, and 1 John 1: 7). This salvation is not automatic to all men but comes only when people such as you have asked Jesus Christ to come into their hearts. Again, we read the words of John: "But to all who received him (Jesus Christ) who believed in his name, he gave power to become children of God" (John 1: 12).

The two key words here are believed and received. Believe refers to the acknowledgement that Jesus is the Son of God and one's Savior (see Romans 10:9-10). And receive implies a willingness to follow Jesus in all that the Bible tells us to do and be (John 14:21).

You have, by receiving Christ, removed the penalty of sin from your life, which is spiritual death in hell. You no longer come into the judgment of God as all unbelievers must, but as Jesus said, you have "passed from death to life" (John 5:24).

God no longer even sees you as a sinner, Paul says, "There is therefore now no condemnation for those who are in Christ Jesus" (Romans 8:1). Your sins have not only been forgiven, but God no longer remembers that you have even committed them (Hebrews 8:12).

So welcome to the family of God. Welcome to the

blessings that God gives His children, to the spiritual riches which are in Christ Jesus.

You may want to stop here and let these scriptures sink deeper into your mind as you study them from your Bible.

For God has a vital message to you as a new Christian. There are 4 things He wants you to know, 4 things he wants you to do, and things he wants you to have. Without these things you will not properly grow in your new life in Christ, but with them God's blessings will forever be with you.

4 THINGS GOD WANTS YOU TO KNOW

Now that you've received Christ there are 4 basic things God wants you to know, not only with the intellect, but with your heart and soul: (1) God loves you. (2) You are a new person. (3) You can live victoriously. (4) God is with you each moment of your life. These are basic principles of the Christian experience which should become an innate part of your new life. They are vital to a life of joy and blessing in Christ.

1. GOD LOVES YOU

No matter what turn your life might take, don't ever forget that God really loves you. Many people feel unloved and unwanted, and man can be cold and uncaring. But God loves all men from the most despicable sinner to the purest Christian. He has demonstrated that love by sending His only Son to die for our sins. Remember (John 3:16)? The

Apostle Paul also writes, "God shows his love for us in that while we were yet sinners Christ died for us." (Romans 5:8)

Why would God send His only Son to die a cruel death for wicked men? It is because He loves us and wants us in Heaven with Him. Paul himself once a sinner, illustrates God's love in Titus 3:3-7. "For we ourselves were once foolish, disobedient, led astray, slaves to various passions and pleasures, passing our days in malice and envy, hated by men and hating one another; but when the goodness and loving kindness of God our Savior appeared, he saved us, not because of deeds done by us in righteousness, but in virtue of his own mercy, by the washing of regeneration and renewal in the Holy Spirit, which he poured out upon us richly through Jesus Christ our Savior, so that we might be justified by his grace and become heirs in hope of eternal life."

Is there anything we have done to earn God's love? No! Is there anything we have done to earn salvation? No! It is because of God's great love for us and by His grace that we can have salvation through Jesus Christ.

Don't ever think that God does not love you. His love is steady and sure.

Paul says in Romans 8:38-39 "that nothing can ever separate us from God's love."

God loves you! Think about it! And because He does, He has saved you and called you to a life of blessing in Christ. Salvation is the first gift you have received from

God, but the treasures of His love will bring more gifts to you, both spiritual and material, time and time again.

So, believe it! Act upon it! Experience it! Thank God for it! He loves you!

2. YOU ARE A NEW PERSON

Believe it or not, you are a brand-new person. Through Jesus Christ you have experienced a spiritual birth. Jesus talked about this new birth in the 3 rd Chapter of John, saying that it was necessary for a man to be "born again" in order to enter the kingdom of God. And that is exactly what happens when a person receives Jesus as his Savior. Paul writes, "Therefore, if anyone is in Christ. He is a new creature; the old has passed away, behold, the new has come" (2 Corinthians 5: 17).

What exactly happens when a person experiences a new birth through Christ? Again, we look at the words of Paul. "We know that our old self was crucified with him (Christ) so that the sinful body might be destroyed, and we might no longer be enslaved to sin" (Romans 6:6). The nature of man is sinful, and before you received Christ you could not help but sin. It doesn't matter whether you were a big sinner or a "little" sinner; your nature was bent toward sin. But when Jesus was crucified, He nailed your old sinful nature to the Cross.

In Christ, therefore, you are a new person. You have now taken on the nature of Christ himself. Paul says, " I have been crucified with Christ; it is no longer I who live, but Christ who lives in me; and the life I now live in the flesh I live by faith in the Son of God, who loved me and gave himself for me" (Galatians 2:20). He is your new nature!

That means you now have a desire for righteousness instead of sin. You now have a desire to serve God instead of yourself. You now have a real grasp of what life is all about-living for the purpose God created you. You have been renewed. You are a brand-new person.

3. YOU CAN LIVE VICTORIOUSLY

Because you are a new person, you are now able to conquer every habit of sin.

(NOTE: Turn to I Corinthians 6:9-11 and Galatians 5:16-21 to see what sin is.) This is not to say that you will never sin. In fact, John says that any Christian who says he never sins is simply not telling the truth (study I John 1:8-9). Note that John also points out the willingness of God to quickly forgive our sins when we are truly repentant.

But God wants us to eliminate our habits of sin. And because Jesus Christ nailed our old sinful natures to the Cross, we can, through Christ and only through Christ, live victoriously above sin.

Then Paul tells us not to yield ourselves to sin, but to yield ourselves to God. Dedicate your spirit, your mind, and your body to God. Devote yourself to serving Him. Paul says that if you do that, sin will have no power over you (read Romans 6:12 and also Ephesians 4:22-24).

So, stand up in the power you have in Christ. Yield yourself to Him, and you will not be overcome by sin.

"The return you get," Paul says, "is eternal life in Christ Jesus our Lord" (Romans 6:22-23).

4. GOD IS WITH YOU EACH MOMENT OF YOUR LIFE

At times it will seem as though God is a million miles away. But He's not.

Jesus said He would never leave us nor forsake us (Matthew 28:20). Furthermore, He said, "If a man loves me, he will keep my word, and my Father will love him, and we will come to him and make our home with him" (John 14:23).

God is always with us. He is faithful. You may slip and fail Him from time to time, but He will still be faithful to you. Many scriptures attest to God's faithfulness (read Psalms 23:4, I Corinthians 1, I Thessalonians 5: 23-24 and II Thessalonians 3:3). Perhaps the classic statement on God's faithfulness to us is found in Deuteronomy 7:9 God said, "Know therefore that the Lord your God is God, the faithful God who keeps covenant and steadfast love with those who love him and keep his commandments, to a thousand generations."

No matter what you may feel like, God is present with

you at all times, for He is faithful. Trust Him. Acknowledge His presence. You can depend upon Him.

Now that you've studied the four things God wants you to know, let's review them: (1) God loves you. (2) You are a new person. (3) You can live victoriously. (4) God is with you each moment of your life. As you incorporate these basic principles into your life, you are well on your way to becoming a mature and happy Christian.

4 THINGS GOD WANTS YOU TO DO. LET'S CIRCLE THE BASES (PICTURE YOURSELF IN A BASEBALL DIAMOND)

Christianity is first of all being. Some people have the mistaken notion that if they do enough good deeds God will consider them Christians. In actuality that is not true. Ephesians 2:8-9 tells us that we are not saved by works, but by faith in Christ. Paul goes on to say that because we have been transformed, we will by virtue of our new natures perform good works. So, doing good deeds follows being.

But in this chapter the "doing" focuses not on good deeds, but actions which will help you grow as a Christian so that you will live a Godly life. (1) Study your Bible. (2) Pray. (3) Fellowship with Christians. (4) Witness for Christ. Each one of these four things God wants you to do is essential to healthy growth as a new person in Christ.

1. STUDY YOUR BIBLE. FIRST BASE

The Bible is the Word of God, and the Word of God

is a very important source of spiritual food. The Apostle Peter, instructing new Christians such as yourself, said, "Like newborn babes long for the pure spiritual milk, and spiritual growth generally occurs in direct relationship to Bible Study.

How does one begin to study the Bible? First of all, if you do not already have a good Bible, invest in one. You will soon treasure it as your most valuable possession. There are many versions to choose from, but it is important that you begin Bible study with modern edition such as The New International Version, The Revised Standard Version, The New American Standard Bible or Amplified Bible. They are much easier to understand than the King James, and all represent vast improvements of older versions.

Once you have a good Bible, you will notice that it is divided into Old and New Testaments. The Old Testament was written before the time of Christ and relates to God's dealings with the Israelites and mankind in general from the day of Creation. The New Testament contains books on the life of Jesus and letters from various apostles of the first century, most of which were written to new Christians throughout the Mediterranean and Asian areas of the world. In as much as we are living in the New Testament age, the place for you to begin to study is there, and not in the Old Testament. A good book to start with is the Gospel of Mark, which is a narrative on the life of Jesus. From there go to the books   1 Corinthians and 1 John, two of the most exciting letters on practical Christianity.

How much should you read at one time? That depends on you. The emphasis is on the Bible study, not just reading. Paul tells us to understand the Word (2Timothy 2: 15), and so it is important that you digest the words of the Bible and not simply read them.

Therefore, how much you read any one time is up to you. A good rule of thumb is to read at least a chapter or two per day. Your own reading habits may indicate more or less. But however, much you read at one sitting, get into the habit of studying the Bible each day. There is no better way to mature as a Christian. The application of God's Word to your life will soon amaze you with the power and love of our wonderful God and our Savior Jesus Christ.

2. PRAY SECOND BASE

Prayer is communication with God. Just as we need to communicate with family, friends, and business associates to foster healthy relationships, we also need to communicate with God to build a strong relationship with Him.

What is the nature of prayer? Some people think prayer is just asking God for things we want. But it is more than that. Paul gives us a perfect illustration of the nature of prayer in Philippians 4:6. He says, "Have no anxiety about anything, but in everything by prayer and supplication with thanksgiving let your requests be made known to God."

Prayer is not only petition, that is, asking God for what we need, but it is also worship. It is time of thanksgiving, when we need to express our appreciation to God for all He has done for us. We enjoy saying "thank you" to someone who has done something for us. Likewise, when we thank God for His blessings the very act of giving thanks precipitates a release of joy in our hearts. And just as we like hearing "thank you" from others, so does God appreciate His children thanking and praising Him. Try it right now Take a moment and thank God for the salvation He has given you from your sins through Jesus Christ. You will experience a joy that is distinctive of the Christian life.

There is also power in prayer. James 5:16 says, "The prayer of a righteous man has great power in its effects." From cover to cover the Bible is laced with stories of great achievements by mortal men who through prayer trusted God. Your life can tell the same story.

How often should you pray? Paul says simply, "Pray constantly" (1 Thess. 5:17). In other words, it is your privilege to talk to God whenever and wherever. You do not have to be in church to pray. Nor should you wait until an emergency arises to pray. Rather, it is a good idea not only to communicate with God throughout the day, but also to set aside a designated time period each day for prayer.

So, get in the habit of talking to God. Pray for your own needs and for others. Praise God for His goodness and love and mercy. Prayer makes a difference even in the life of the most mature Christian. It will make a difference in yours. As you experience answered prayer you will grow into a solid, dynamic person for Jesus Christ.

3. FELLOWSHIP WITH CHRISTIANS
THIRD BASE

Regular church attendance is very important, especially for a new Christian. You will need the fellowship and encouragement of other Christians as you grow in Christ. That is why the book of Hebrews tells us, "let us consider how to stir up one another to love and good works, not neglecting to meet together, as is the habit of some, but encouraging one another" (Hebrews 10: 24,25).

Much of the help you will receive in your Christian walk will come from Christian friends. Paul writes that we are to bear one another's burdens (Galatians 6:2), and often God chooses to minister to us through the love and prayers of fellow Christians.

So, it is very important that you establish a habit of church attendance. No one can choose a church for you, only God can do that. But it should be a church where there is love and concern, and where the Bible is faithfully taught as the Word of God.

If you are not yet acquainted with a church in your neighborhood, first ask God to help you find one and then investigate several for yourself until you locate a place where you feel at home. And then watch how much God will bless you as you pray, sing praises to Him, and fellowship with other people who have found the joy of knowing Christ as Savior and Lord.

4. WITNESS FOR CHRIST. HOME PLATE

To be a witness for Christ simply means to tell others what Jesus has done for you. In the Gospel of John there was a man named Andrew whom Jesus called to be one of His twelve Apostles. The first thing Andrew did after heeding the call of Jesus was to go tell his brother, Simon Peter, that he had found the Messiah the Jews had been looking for (John 1:40-42). Peter also became one of Jesus Apostles.

A witness is one who testifies or gives evidence to that which he has seen or experienced. You can witness to others by both your words and your deeds. Sometimes the greatest witness is by deed. One who has received Christ and become a changed person is dynamic witness to his friends.

But God also wants us to witness with our tongues. Think about someone you can share your experience with, someone who does not know Jesus. It might be a friend or relative, perhaps someone in your immediate family. Ask God to help you witness to that person. He will!

Obviously, witnessing about Jesus is a benefit to those who have been witnessed to. Had not someone witnessed to you about Jesus you would not be a Christian today.

But there is another benefit of witnessing. You receive a spiritual blessing just from sharing Jesus Christ with another person. The person may not even accept Jesus as you did. In fact, you will run into some people who will laugh at you for believing in Jesus. But witnessing is a spiritual experience that brings joy and strength to the inner being of a Christian. Try It! You will be surprised how it will strengthen your faith and determination to follow Christ.

So, there you have it, four things Gods wants to do. Let's review them again: (1) Study your Bible. (2) Pray. (3) Fellowship with Christians. (4) Witness for Christ. All are valuable and necessary for Christian growth. If you haven't started doing, get started today, and you will be thrilled at how the doing of these four things will add greatly to your being. So, let's run around the bases!

4 THINGS GOD WANTS YOU TO HAVE.

God not only wants you to know and to do, but it also having. There are many things we can have in Christ, but basically there are four precious things God wants to give us. (1) Peace. (2) The Baptism in the Holy Spirit. (3) A better life. (4) Heaven.

1. PEACE

The only way a person can ever have peace in his soul is through Christ.

In scripture God is often referred to as the "God of peace," and the very reason Jesus came was to bring peace to mankind (Acts 10:36).

The kind of peace God wants you to have most of all is spiritual peace, peace of the soul. Paul says, "Therefore, since we are justified by faith, we have peace with God through our Lord Jesus Christ" (Romans 5:1). Paul is talking about the peace one has from knowing that his sins are forgiven. You see, you no longer stand in the judgment of God, for Christ has already made atonement for your sins.

So, rest in God's peace. It is yours today by your faith in Christ.

Not only does Jesus give us peace about the destiny of our souls, but He also gives us peace in temporal situations. In John 14:27 He said, "Peace I leave with you; my peace I give to you; not as the world gives do, I give to you. Let not your hearts be troubled, neither let them be afraid." And in John 16:33 He adds, "In me you may have peace. In the world you have tribulation; but be of good cheer, I have overcome the world."

Though the storms of life may be raging about you, you can have peace knowing that God is with you and that He will help you. It is a peace that comes through prayer by the grace of God, and it is a peace you can find only in Christ. Paul's prayer for the Thessalonians are words to remember: "Now may the Lord of peace himself give you peace at all times in all ways" (IL Thessalonians 3: 16).

When you are perplexed over life's trying circumstances, stop and study Philippians 4:4-7. Then pray and God will give you a peace in your heart and mind that will strengthen you and see you through.

2. THE BAPTISM IN THE HOLY SPIRIT.

You first received the Holy Spirit in your life the moment you accepted Christ as your Savior. But there is yet another experience of the Holy Spirit which is distinct from salvation, and it is referred to in scripture as the Baptism in the Holy Spirit (see Mark I :8, Acts 1:4-5, and Acts 11:16).

Baptism literally means "immersion," and so when one is baptized in the Holy Spirit he is literally immersed in the power and presence of the Spirit. In this experience the Holy Spirit actually indwells a person. Many times, it is said of people in the scriptures that they are "filled" with the Spirit.

Basically, this experience is for the power that we might be witnesses of Christ both in word and in deed. In Acts 1:8 Jesus told His Apostles that they would receive power to be His witnesses when they were baptized with the Holy Spirit (study verses 1 to 8). In I Corinthians 12 Paul gives us a list of spiritual gifts which are given by the Holy Spirit to Christians who have received this infilling. These gifts are given to help us witness to non-Christians, and to minister to others, but that God might minister to us as well. When one is filled with Spirit, he has more power to serve God, a greater joy and love for Christ, and a deeper prayer life. Every Christian needs to be baptized in the Holy Spirit.

How can you receive this blessed experience? It can be received simply by prayer and asking God for it (study Luke 1 1:9-13). However, in the days of the early Church it was generally received through the prayers of others who had already received the experience.

Don't delay, this experience is for you. It will help you be a stronger Christian and make you a powerful witness for Christ.

3. A BETTER LIFE.

Some people believe that Christianity is a drab, depressing life of hardship and deprivation. Actually, Christianity is just the opposite- it is an exciting life, a better life than any non-Christian can have. That is not to say that God will make you a millionaire (although He has done just that for some Christians!) But God has promised you a life of blessing.

First of all, there are spiritual blessings. Your life is now one of peace and one that is free from the enslaving power of sin. You will receive great satisfaction not only in your mind but also in your spirit by serving Christ.

Secondly, Christianity is a life of physical blessings. Sin often shows its ravaging effects in our bodies, but one who is free from sin is a healthier person. But over and above that, we have a God who delights in healing our sick bodies. Untold thousands have been healed through prayer-not by man's doing, but by the mercy and power of God.

Third, God does want to bless us materially. One who desires to serve Christ will find that material "things" are not that important anymore, but God has promised to supply all our needs when we seek His kingdom and give ourselves to Him (see Matthew 6:31-33 and Philippians 4:19).

4. HEAVEN.

The grand climax of the Christian experience is spending eternity in the presence of God and in the riches and treasures of His kingdom. Paul says, "No eye has seen, nor ear heard, nor the heart of man conceived, what God has prepared for those who love him." (I Corinthians 2:9).

What exactly is Heaven like? God gives us only a glimpse into Heaven. In Revelation the Apostle John was given a vision of Heaven. And he says that he heard a voice, which said of Heaven, "Behold, the dwelling of God is with men. He will dwell with them, and they shall be his people, and God himself will be with them; he will wipe away every tear from their eyes, and death shall be no more, neither shall there be mourning nor crying nor pain any more, for the former things have passed away" (Revelation 21 : 1-4). How different than life on this earth!

Furthermore, Heaven is described as a paradise with streets of gold. Whether that is literal or not we cannot be sure, but Heaven is unlike anything man now knows. Heaven is the end of sorrow and suffering. Heaven is experiencing the joys and riches of God forever. And God wants you to be there!

What a precious and loving God we have, who delights

in giving. Let's review again the things He wants us to have: (1) Peace. (2) The Baptism of the Holy Spirit. (3) A better Life. (4) Heaven.

Don't miss a thing God has for you. Be everything He wants you to be and do everything He wants you to do. And in the being and doing you shall have all that He wants to give you.

Aren't you glad that you made the decision to receive Christ as your Savior? God has and exciting life for you in the days ahead. You will be eternally grateful that God sent Jesus Christ to die for your sins and that you decided to receive Him and serve Him.

So again, welcome to the family of God, and may, as the Apostle Paul prays, "The grace of the Lord Jesus Christ and the love of God and the fellowship of the Holy Spirit be with you" (II Corinthians 13:14).

DISCIPLES PRAYER MANUAL

APOSTLE RAY GIMINEZ

INTRODUCTION

DISCIPLES PRAYER MANUAL

Sometimes it's hard to find answers just when we need them the most. I believe that praying scriptures will empower the believer and enhance his spiritual development in Christ. "See the Lord watches over His Word to perform it." (Jeremiah 1:12). We need an encounter with Jesus Christ and through prayer He will forgive our sins and heal our land. Our inadequacies in our Christian walk are due to prayerlessness. We are handicapped because at times we don't stand behind His Word and claim it.

This manual has been prepared to be of service to hungry Christians, so that they can keep focused on the Word. I have taken the Scriptures from the NIV version and made them personal by replacing the word "you" with "I" or "me. " This is not a new concept, but it will implement vital habits that will destroy the enemy strategies against you and bring you closer to the Master.

I have also outlined prayers against curses, prayers for our country, and even explained what spiritual warfare really is. You will be exposed to the different types of fast as mentioned in the Bible and able to understand why fasting and prayer sometimes go together so well.

There is also a segment that explains the very exciting new method of meditating with God called "Soaking."

All these different types of prayers and explanations will release ministering spirits that will aid in your conflict and need. I pray this manual will be a service to you as we labor for the King.

> *"If my people, who are called by My name, will humble themselves and pray and seek My face and turn from their wicked ways, then I will hear from heaven and will forgive their sin and heal their land." (2 Chronicles 7:14-15)*

INSTRUCTIONS FOR USING THE PRAYER MANUAL

The tribe of Issachar (1 Chronicles 12:32) it is said in the scriptures that "They understood the times and knew what to do." As Christians in the body of Christ we must understand we're living in very different times (as preferred in the Bible) and we must understand that only prayers will prevail against the forces of Evil. By simply vocalizing the prayers related, you will be empowered to win every battle facing you, your family, your region, your nation. The essence of prayer is a personal relationship with God. We ascend with Him to heavenly places as we pray, and we descend with His anointing over our lives and the details of His work to do on this earth.

This manual has instructions on spiritual warfare, fasting, prayers on being freed from curses. It gives detailed prayers for our country. This manual teaches you how to meditate on God through the method of soaking. But most of all, you will know how to vocalize prayers for your benefit.

Through this Prayer Manual you will have a greater appreciation and understanding of God's word. Your prayer life will be enhanced as the scripture passages begin to be lodged into your memory. The manual is designed to help you see how God will answer your prayers as you make these confessions of how the Lord is influencing your life through the answered prayers.

It is my prayer that this manual becomes a very helpful tool to you, and that the blessing and outpouring of God's Spirit will fall upon you as you enter into His Kingdom.

In His Service,

Ray Gimenez

SPIRITUAL WARFARE

WHAT IS SPIRITUAL WARFARE

It is a cosmic-earthly conflict. It is the Kingdom of God and the Kingdom of Evil. Supernatural forces that are engaged in fierce conflict against one another. It can be said that it is the struggle between good and evil – the battle between right and wrong or between light and darkness. It can be referred to as the conflict between the positive forces which seek to preserve life and order in the universe, and the negative which tend to disturb and even destroy life and order. But even though this is a present reality, such was not the case in the beginning, nor will it be so in the future. "In the beginning God…" is the view of Scripture. There was no evil, no opposing force; only God, and God is good. Then God created moral beings, the angels and placed them within His Kingdom; they obeyed His will. At some point, however in the hidden past, rebellion occurred within the angel's Kingdom. Immediately, two kingdoms were born. Evil entered God's Kingdom, dividing it into two, the kingdom of God and the kingdom of Satan. But as we focus on Scripture we move through time from the "eternal" past to the "eternal" future, then Satan's Kingdom vanishes. The ultimate state is secured in the Scriptures. Only God and His perfect Kingdom will exist in the eternal future. Until then from a biblical perspective we are engaged in an on-going conflict waged on two fronts: God and His angel's Kingdom confront Satan and his demon's Kingdom. While the children of God contend with the children of Satan we must understand how to prevail in spiritual warfare.

LEVELS OF SPIRITUAL WARFARE

GROUND - LEVEL SPIRITUAL WARFARE

This ministry involves casting demons out of people. It was practiced by Jesus and has been a part of many Christian Churches throughout the centuries. It involves deliverance ministries.

OCCULT - LEVEL SPIRITUAL WARFARE

This ministry deals with demonic forces unleashed through activities related to Satanism, witchcraft, Freemasonry, Eastern religions, New Age, shamanism, astrology and many other forms of structural occultism. The demonic powers at work in many cases are significantly different than those operating on ground level.

STRATEGIC - LEVEL SPIRITUAL WARFARE

This ministry describes confrontation with high-ranking principalities and powers much like Paul writes about in Ephesians 6:12. These enemy forces are frequently called "territorial spirits" because they attempt to keep large numbers of humans networked through cities, nations, neighborhoods, people, communities, religious alliances, industries or any other form of society in spiritual captivity. This level of warfare is also called "cosmic-level spiritual warfare."

SOAKING IN GOD'S PRESENCE

WHAT IS SOAKING

REST AND RESTORATION

Soaking is a Psalm 23 experience. "He makes us to lie down in green pastures and He leads us by still waters. He restores our soul. " As part of the restoration process we may find ourselves responding physically or emotionally. We might laugh, cry, or shake as the Holy Spirit works in us. The Holy Spirit might give us a vision or bring a memory to mind that He wants to heal. Often, we enter into a deep rest, even falling asleep. Even if we don't feel anything happening, we believe that the Lord is working in our spirit.

CHILD-LIKE FAITH

Soaking is a dedication: "God, this is time just for you."

Soaking is an invitation: "God, do what you want to in me."

Soaking is an expectation: "Thank you Father for what you are accomplishing as I rest in you." We come to Him like little children believing that He has good things for us. "If you then.... know how to give good gifts to your children how much more will your Heavenly Father give the Holy Spirit to them that ask Him."

ABIDE IN THE VINE

Intimacy with God is the key to fruitfulness in every area of our lives. As we become more aware of His presence in us ... so do other people. As we become more affected by His presence in us ... so do those around us. By taking time in the secret place with God, we start to walk by the spirit in everyday life. We find that rather than striving to achieve things for God, He is building His Kingdom through us. "Not by might, not by power, but by His Spirit."

HUMAN BEINGS (NOT DOINGS)

At first, we may have an internal Mary/Martha struggle. We feel like a Martha that we should be "doing" something, but this is a Mary time. Martha got caught up in the busyness of serving Jesus; Mary got caught up in Him. Soaking is not about how much we can accomplish by our own efforts; it's about God's action in us.

HOW TO SOAK

QUIET TIME

A peaceful environment on the outside helps us to come to peace on the inside. When we soak, we simply put on some quiet instrumental or worship music and lie down. At first our minds will be whirring with thoughts, but we don't try and wrestle them. We just wait for them to settle, submitting our mind to the Holy Spirit. Meditating on the fact that the Lord is in our spirits, we believe He is right there with us. If we get distracted, we don't become frustrated, we just simply turn our attention back to the Lord.

- Find a comfortable place to lie down
- Put on some soaking music
- Allow the busyness of your thoughts to quiet down (don't fight them)
- Invite the Holy Spirit to soak you in His presence
- Pray and surrender yourself to the Holy Spirit – mind, body and soul
- Focus on the Lord's presence in you
- Rest in faith, believing He is working in you
- Take as much time as you can (Try to give yourself as least 20 minutes to start to relax and receive)
- Get up refreshed and full of the Holy Spirit

- Watch as God changes you and the world around you
- Just Relax

One of the main barriers to encountering God is that we are simply trying too hard. God's top tip to us is "just relax". In Psalm 46:10, He puts it this way, "Be still and know that I am God. " Literally translated, this means "Cease striving and know that I am God." The way to know God is through peace and stillness.

SCRIPTURES FOR SOAKING

- Rest in the Lord and wait patiently for Him. (Psalm 37:7)

- ...Meditate within your heart on your bed and be still. (Psalm 4:4)

- Come to Me, all you who labor and are heavy laden, and I will give you rest. Take My yoke upon you and learn from Me, for I am gentle and lowly in heart, and you will find rest for your souls. For My yoke is easy and My burden is light." (Matthew 11:28-30)

- There remains therefore a rest for the people of God. For he who has entered His rest has himself also ceased from His word as God did from His. Let us therefore be diligent to enter that rest. (Hebrews 4:9-11)

- Be still and know that I am God. (Psalm 46:10)

- He gives power to the weak, and to those who have no might. He increases strength. Even the youth shall faint and be weary, and the young men shall utterly fall, but those who wait on the Lord shall renew their strength. They shall run and not be weary. They shall walk and not faint. (Isaiah 40:29-31)

- Wait on the Lord. Be of good courage, and He shall strengthen your heart. Wait, I say, on the Lord! (Psalm 27:14)

- The Lord is my shepherd. I shall not want. He makes me lie down in green pastures. He leads me beside the still waters. He restores my soul. (Psalm 23:1- 3)

- And she had a sister called Mary who also sat at Jesus' feet and heard His word. (Luke 10:39)

SHORT SELECTION OF SOAKING MUSIC

- Laura Woodley – www.spiritsoulbody.com

- Alberto and Kimberly Rivera – www. rainingpresence.com

- Ruth Fazal – www.ruthfazal.com

FASTING

WHAT IS YOUR BODY TRYING TO TELL YOU?

For starters, ask yourself this question: Are you listening to your body? Do you understand what it's trying to tell you? Sickness and degenerative disease are usually simply nature's way of telling you that your body is toxic and needs to be cleansed. If you were driving your car and the red engine light came on indicating that it was time to check the engine, would you continue to drive the car without taking it to the shop to have it checked? This actually happened to a patient. She ended up having to replace her engine because she ignored the red light.

You may laugh, as her family members did when she told me the story. However, this is exactly what many of us are doing. Our red engine light is flashing through the symptoms and signs of degenerative diseases that we are experiencing – diabetes, heart disease, arthritis, headaches, allergies, psoriasis, rheumatoid arthritis, lupus and other degenerative diseases.

Too often we simply ignore the signs and symptoms and continue eating the wrong foods. We also keep living our stressed-out, unhealthy lifestyles of cigarette smoking, drinking alcohol and not exercising.

Our bodies simply weren't designed to handle it all. Nevertheless, we continue to push and stress our bodies with these toxic burdens until they eventually develop diseases. At that point, we then run to the doctor and get medication, which further strains the liver's ability to detoxify and does nothing to cleanse it.

If this sounds like you, chances are you are simply toxic and probably overfed. Simply beefing up your intake of supplements usually won't help. So, what can you do?

The answer is fasting. Fasting is a powerful, natural way to cleanse your body from the burden of excess toxic nutrients, such as bad fats, and from all other chemicals and toxins that cause degenerative diseases.

Fasting is the safest and best way to heal the body from degenerative diseases caused by being overfed with the wrong nutrition.

Fasting cleanses and rejuvenates the body physically, mentally and spiritually. It is also one of the best ways of preventing and treating sickness and disease, as we will see later.

The ancient father of medicine, Hippocrates, said, "Everything in excess is opposed by nature." Our nation is suffering an epidemic of degenerative diseases and death that is caused by excess pain. We have eaten too much sugar, too much fat, too many empty calories and far too much processed, devitalized food.

PERIODIC FASTING

Periodic fasting, followed by a cleansing diet, will allow you to live free of the physical and neurological burden of toxins. Fasting gives your toxic, overtaxed body an opportunity to "catch up" with its overwhelming task of waste removal. Periodic, short-term fasting will also strengthen your immune system and help you live longer.

GENERAL BENEFITS OF FASTING

Fasting gives a rest to the digestive tract. Your body uses a significant amount of your energy every day in digesting, absorbing and assimilating your food. Since fresh juices are very easy for the body to assimilate, they give your digestive tract a chance to rest and repair. This, in turn, gives your overburdened liver a chance to catch up on its work of detoxification.

RELIEF THROUGH FASTING

Finding toxic relief through fasting can turn your life and

health around. It is a natural, biblical system of supporting and cleansing the body from built-up chemicals, fats and other toxins. It also has amazing spiritual benefits, as we will see later on.

NATURAL PRINCIPLE OF HEALING

Fasting allows your body to heal by giving it a rest. All living things need to rest, including you. Even the land must rest, which was a principle God gave to the ancient agrarian Jewish nation regarding their fields. Every seventh year they followed that system so it could reestablish its own mineral and nutrient content.

FASTING ENERGIZES CELLS

Fasting is also an energy booster. The toxic buildup in the cells congests the mitochondria (the energy factories in each cell) so they cannot effectively produce energy. This leads to fatigue, irritability and lethargy. Mitochondria are sites within each of your cells where energy is produced. Metabolic waste, chemicals and other toxins affect the function of the mitochondria of the cell, making them less efficient in producing energy.

REJUVENATE PHYSICALLY, MENTALLY AND SPIRITUALLY

Deep cleansing of every cell in your body through fasting has the wonderful added benefit of improving your appearance. As your body detoxifies, your skin will eventually become clearer and glow with a radiance that you probably haven't seen for quite a few years. The whites of your eyes usually become clearer and whiter and may even sparkle. As toxic fat melts away through fasting, you'll feel and look better than you have in years. Your energy will be supercharged. And your mental functioning usually improves as your body cleanses, repairs and rejuvenates.

THE WHY OF SPIRITUAL FASTING

So why should we fast? What does denying ourselves our favorite foods actually do for us?

BUILDS GODLY CHARACTER

By enabling us to surrender our lives to God in greater measure, we find more control over our tongues, our minds, our attitudes, our emotions, our bodies and all our fleshly desires. Fasting also helps us to submit our spirits to God completely so that He can use them for His purposes.

It really is possible to be led by the spirit of God and not be ruled by fleshly desires. However, even though many Christians have invited the power of the Holy Spirit into their lives, they continue to be led about by the insatiable appetites of the flesh. They live their lives pursuing whatever gratifies the cravings of the lower nature or their own selfish motives instead of the purposes of God. Many are good people who actually would like to live on a much higher plane of existence, but they just don't know how.

Fasting allows us to die to the appetites of the lower

nature, to the lusts of the flesh. It gives us the ability to build up character and integrity by allowing the Spirit of God to operate through us. The only real way to build Godly character and genuine integrity into our inner man is by spending time in the presence of God.

FIND THE PRESENCE OF GOD

Have you ever desired to experience God's presence? Fasting can bring the healing and refreshing presence of God into an individual life and into the life of a family or even a nation. Too many of us let natural things absorb our time and energy when we could be enjoying the glorious realm of God's Spirit.

After Moses fasted for forty days, he was swept up into an entirely new place in God's Spirit. He received the Ten Commandments and became the lawgiver of Israel. After Jesus had fasted for forty days, the Holy Spirit empowered His life, and His ministry of healing and preaching was launched.

You too can receive the touch of God's glory upon your own life, just as Jesus and Moses did, through fasting and prayer. The kind of prayer that simply makes long lists of requests to God is not enough. You must enter into the realm of the Holy Spirit through worship, reading God's words and listening to God's voice as well as making requests.

Moses experienced the same hunger for more of God that you may be experiencing right now. He prayed that

God might reveal Himself to him, although no man could actually look at God and live. His request is found in Exodus 33. The Lord then instructed him:

> And the Lord said, "Here is a place by me, and you shall stand on the rock. So, it shall be, while My glory passes by, that I will put you in the cleft of the rock, and will cover you with My hand while I pass by. Then I will take away My hand, and you shall see My back; but My face shall not be seen." Exodus 33:21-23

In other words, Moses got a glance of the glory of the back of God.

TYPES OF FASTING

CORPORATE FASTING - FOR THE FORGIVENESS OF SINS

Historically, God's people were commanded to fast once a year. On the Day of Atonement, all Israel came before God in corporate fasting and repentance. (See Leviticus 16:29-34; 23:26-32)

The Day of Atonement was considered the single most sacred day of the entire religious year. A day in which everyone in the entire nation stopped everything they were doing. They refused to eat and sought God's forgiveness for all the sins committed that year.

Leviticus 16:29 tells us: "This shall be a statue forever to you: In the seventh month, on the tenth day of the month, you shall afflict your souls, and do no work at all."

THE ESTHER FAST - FOR PROTECTION, DELIVERANCE, AND DIVINE FAVOR

Esther was a beautiful, young Hebrew girl living in Persia during Israel's captivity. This lovely woman was chosen as queen over all the other young women in the entire nation. The prime minister of Persia was Haman, an evil man who hated the Jews. Haman succeeded in passing a law of genocide to kill all the Jews. Therefore, Queen Esther decided to risk going before the king to try and save her people. According to the laws, if anyone, even the queen, requested an uninvited audience with the king, that person could be killed.

Faced with the danger to her people and the danger to Esther herself, the queen called a fast. The Bible says:

> *"Go, gather together all Jews who are in Susa, and fast for me. Do not eat or drink for three days and three days, night or day. I and my maids will fast as you do. When this is done, I will go to the king, Even though it is against the law. And if I perish, I perish." Esther 4:16*

THE EZRA FAST - FOR DIRECTION AND PROTECTION

For centuries the nation of Jews was held in captivity by the nation of Persia. When freedom finally came, Ezra, a priest, was given permission by Cyrus, the king of Persia, to return to Jerusalem to rebuild the magnificent Jerusalem temple. The trip to Jerusalem was very dangerous. Ezra needed protection to lead the great caravan of thousands of defenseless Jews back to their home city. He was ashamed to ask the God's protection for all who worship Him. Many of the travelers actually had become wealthy in captivity, and so Ezra was responsible for safely transporting their treasures and other belongings as well.

> *Ezra 8:21 says, "I proclaimed a fast, so that we might humble ourselves before our God and ask him for a safe journey for us and our children, with all our possessions."*

They fasted for the protection, security and direction from God. The journeyers returned to Israel in safety with all of their possessions intact. Once again, the Bible reports powerful spiritual results were obtained through fasting.

THE ELIJAH FAST - FOR COMBATING SPIRITUAL ENEMIES

Although corporate fasting was common, individual fasts were even more so. Elijah was another spiritual giant of the Bible who understood the power of fasting for affecting the outcome of great spiritual battles. The Elijah fast is undertaken during times of intense spiritual conflict.

Elijah had just won the greatest victory of his life over four hundred fifty prophets of Baal. He actually had called fire down from heaven and then had all of those demonically inspired prophets of Baal killed. Queen Jezebel, who had given these prophets a place of authority, responded in an angry frenzy, threatening to murder Elijah by the very next day.

Thrown into a state of terror, depression and despondency, Elijah ran for his life. He didn't stop running until he was about a day's journey away in the wilderness, where he sat down to rest under a juniper tree. It seems clear that Elijah realized that he lacked what it took to battle what was coming against him. In I Kings 19:5-8, we read:

> *"Then as he lay and slept under a broom [juniper] tree, Suddenly an angel touched him, and said to him, "Arise and eat." Then he looked, and there by his head was a cake Baked on coals, and a jar of water. So, he ate and drank, and lay down again. And the angel of the Lord came back the second time, And touched him, and said, "Arise and eat, because the journey is too great for you." So he arose, and ate and drank; And he went in the strength of that food forty days and forty nights As far as Horeb, the mountain of God."*

THE DANIEL FAST - FOR OVERCOMING THE FLESH

Daniel and three other Hebrew youths, Shadrach, Meshach and Abednego, were Jews in captivity, in the kingdom of Babylon. They were greatly favored for their purity, and they were well educated and extremely gifted both mentally and spiritually.

When these four young men were captured and taken into the king's palace to educate them in the ways of the Chaldeans, Daniel 1:5 states, "The king assigned them a daily amount of food and wine from the king's table." He planned to keep them on his own rich diet of meats, fats, sugary pastries and wine for three years. At the end of the three years they would be presented to the king.

However, verse 8 says, "But Daniel resolved not to defile himself with the royal food and wine." In other words, Daniel rejected the rich, temptingly delicious meats, wine and pastries of the royal court, perhaps because they did not meet the requirements of Jewish dietary laws, or because these youths may have taken vows against drinking alcohol.

So, Daniel made a request of the prince of the eunuchs. Verse 12 says, "Please test your servants for ten days: give us nothing but vegetables to eat and water to drink" The King James Version uses the word pulse. "Pulse" consisted of vegetables and grains, wheat, barley, rye, peas, beans and lentils. Daniel and the three other Hebrew youths lived a fasted life for three years and 10 days on the vegetarian diet of pulse while learning and studying in the king's court, and God honored their partial fast. We're told in verse 15, "At the end of the ten days they looked healthier and better nourished than any of the young men who ate the royal food."

God tremendously favored their decision to fast and granted them favor, wisdom and insight far above anyone around them. In verses 18-20 we read:

> "At the end of the time set by the king to bring them in, The chief official presented them to Nebuchadnezzar. The king talked with them, and he found none equal to Daniel, Hananiah, Mishael and Azariah. So, they entered the king's service. In every matter of wisdom and understanding About which the king questioned them, He found them ten times better than all the magicians And enchanters in his whole kingdom."

THE DISCIPLES' FAST - FOR EMPOWERED MINISTRY

When the disciples who traveled with Jesus were sent out to begin ministering on their own, they encountered some unexpected resistance to the healing power of God. When the disciples were powerless to heal a young boy, the child's father approached Jesus. The father's request is recorded in Matthew 17:15.

*"Lord, have mercy on my son, for he is an
Epileptic and suffers severely; for he often falls
Into the fire and often into the water."*

Apparently, the father didn't understand that his son was actually gripped by a demonic force. Although most cases of epilepsy have physical causes, this particular case did not.

In Matthew 17:16, we see that the father had taken his son to the disciples, but they were powerless to respond. Many of our own youth, teens and young adults are bound with alcohol, drugs, nicotine, sexual desire, a spirit of revelry and partying, homosexuality, Satanism, witchcraft, palm reading and other dangerous strongholds. Unfortunately, some of these young people are Christians, but they are still bound with fear, anger, bitterness, resentment, unforgiveness, jealousy, strife, envy and many other deadly emotions.

How can our youth be bound with these strongholds and yet profess to know Christ? Here's how. They may have had their sins forgiven, and they may have professed Christ as their Savior, but they have never had the spiritual chains of wickedness broken off of them. Isaiah 58:6 says, "Is this not the fast that I have chosen: to lose the bonds of wickedness, to undo the heavy burdens, to let the oppressed go free, and that you break every yoke?"

The disciples' fast breaks yokes, or breaks mental, spiritual and emotional bondages, and sets people free.

If you are a mother or father with a son or daughter in rebellion, bound with homosexuality, sexual perversion, sexual desire, drugs, alcohol or any other stronghold, Jesus Christ can set them free by applying the principles of the fast of the disciples.

LIVING A FASTED LIFE

Many great ministers with special callings in the Bible actually went beyond fasting. They lived a fasted lifestyle. John the Baptist was one of these individuals who lived his entire life in a partially fasted state. We see this lifestyle described in Matthew 3:4: "And his food was locusts and wild honey."

John the Baptist was a Nazarite. He was called to a Nazarite vow and a fasted life before he was even born. That call is recorded in Luke 1:15

> *"For he will be great in the sight of the Lord,*
> *and shall drink neither wine nor strong drink.*
> *He will also be filled with the Holy Spirit, even*
> *from his mother's womb."*

OLD TESTAMENT SCRIPTURES

1. God said that he will make me into a great nation and will bless me; He will make my name great, and I will be a blessing. (Genesis 12:2)

2. He will bless those who bless me, and whoever

curses me He will curse; and all peoples on earth will be blessed through me. (Genesis 12:3)

3. The Lord will fight for me; I need only to be still. (Exodus 14: 14)

4. God is sending an angel ahead of me to guard me along the way and to bring me to the place He has prepared. (Exodus 23:20)

5. If I fail to do God's will, I will be sinning against the Lord; and I can be sure that my sin will find me out. (Numbers 32:23)

6. I the Lord is He who gives you the ability to produce wealth. (Deuteronomy 8:18)

7. If I fully obey the Lord my God and carefully follow all his commands. He will set me high above all the nations of the earth. (Deuteronomy 28:1)

8. I will be blessed in the city and blessed in the country. (Deuteronomy 28:3)

9. My fruit of my womb will be blessed, and the crops of my land and the young of my livestock-the calves of my herds and the lambs of my flocks, all will be blessed. (OT 28:4)

10. My basket and kneading trough will be blessed. (Deuteronomy 28:5)

11. I will be blessed when I come in and blessed when I go out. (Deuteronomy 28:6)

12. The Lord will grant that the enemies who rise up against me will be defeated before me. They will come at me from one direction but flee from me in seven. (Deuteronomy 28:7)

13. The Lord will send a blessing on my barns and on everything I put my hands to. The Lord my God will bless me in the land He has giving me. (Deuteronomy 28:8)

14. The Lord will establish me as part of his holy people, and He promised me an oath, if I keep his commands and walk in His ways. (Deuteronomy 28:9)

15. When l walk in his ways, all the people on earth will see that I am called by the name of the Lord, and they will fear Him. (Deuteronomy 28:10)

16. The Lord will grant me abundant prosperity. (Deuteronomy 28:11)

17. The Lord will open the heavens, the store house of his bounty, to send rain on my land in season and to bless all the work of my hands. (Deuteronomy 28:12)

18. I will lend to many nations and borrow from none. (Deuteronomy 28:12)

19. The Lord will make me the head and not the tail. (Deuteronomy 28:13)

20. I will always be at the top, never at the bottom. (Deuteronomy 28:13)

21. The secret things belong to the Lord my God, but the things revealed belong to me and to my children forever, that I may follow all the words of his law. (Deuteronomy 29:29)

22. I will be strong and courageous. I will not be afraid or terrified, for the Lord my God goes with me, He will never leave me nor forsake me. (Deuteronomy 31:6)

23. I will not allow this book of the law depart from my mouth. I will meditate on it day and night, and I will be very careful to do everything written in it. Then I will be prosperous and successful. (Joshua 1:8)

24. This day I choose for myself whom I will serve ... "As for me and my household, I will serve the Lord." (Joshua 24:15)

25. For me to obey is better than sacrifice. (1 Samuel 15:12)

26. The Lord does not look at my outward appearance, but the Lord looks at my heart. (1 Samuel 16:7)

27. I know that God's way is perfect; His word is flawless, He is my shield when I take refuge in him. (2 Samuel 12:31)

28. I will observe what the Lord my God requires: Walk

in his ways and keep his decrees and commands, His laws and requirements, then I will prosper in all I do and wherever I go. (1 Kings 2:3)

29. Just like Elijah did, I will not waver between two opinions. I know the Lord is God and I will follow Him. (1 Kings 18:21)

30. I will worship the Lord my God; and He will deliver me from the hand of all my enemies. (2 Kings 17:39

31. I will cry out as Jabez cried out! "Oh, that you would bless me and enlarge my territory". Let your hand be with me, and keep me from harm so that I will be free from pain. I know that God will grant my request. (1 Chronicles 4:10)

32. I will look to the Lord and his strength, and seek His face always. (1 Chronicles 16:4)

33. Yours, O Lord, is the greatness and the power, and the glory and the majesty and the splendor, for everything in heaven and earth is yours. (1 Chronicles 29:11)

34. I am called by His name, so I will humble myself and pray and seek His face and turn from my wicked ways, then I will hear from heaven and He will forgive my sin and heal my land. (1 Chronicles 7:14)

35. When I fast and petition God, He will answer my prayers. (Ezra 8:23)

36. The joy of the Lord is my strength. (Nehemiah 8:10)

37. Lord you have given me life and showed me your kindness, and in your providence, you watch over my spirit. (Job 10:12)

38. To God belongs wisdom and power, counsel and understanding. (Job 12:13)

39. I will submit to God and be at peace with Him: In this way prosperity will come to me. I will accept instruction from His mouth and lay up His words in my heart. (Job 22:21-22)

40. God knows the way that I take; and when He tests me, I will come forth as gold. (Job 23:10)

41. I know that the fear of the Lord is wisdom, and to shun evil is understanding. (Job 28:18)

42. God's eyes are upon my ways; He sees my every step. (Job 34:21)

43. I am blessed when I choose not to walk in the counsel of the wicked or stand in the way of sinners or sit in the seat of mockers. (Psalms 1:1)

44. I consider your heavens, the work of your fingers, the moon and the stars, which you have set in place, and I know that you are mindful of me. (Psalms 3-4)

45. The words of the Lord are flawless, like silver refined in a furnace of clay, purified seven times. (Psalms 12:6)

46. I love you, O Lord, my strength. (Psalms 18: 1)

47. The Lord is my rock, my fortress and my deliverer; My God is my rock, in whom I take refuge. He is my shield and the horn of my salvation, my stronghold. (Psalms 18:2)

48. I call to the Lord, who is worthy of praise, and I am saved from my enemies. (Psalms 18:3)

49. In my distress I call to the Lord; and I cry out for His help. From His temple He heard my voice. My cry came before Him, into his ears. (Psalms 18:6)

50. For I have kept the ways of the Lord; I have not done evil by turning from God. (Psalms 18:21)

51. All his laws are before me; I have not turned away from his decrees. (Psalms 18:22)

52. I have been blameless before Him and have kept myself from sin. (Psalms 18:23)

53. The Lord has rewarded me according to my righteousness, according to the cleanness of my hands in His sight. (Psalms 18:24)

54. It is God who arms me with strength and makes my way perfect. (Psalms 18:32)

55. He makes my feet like the feet of a deer; He enables me to stand on the heights. (Psalms 18:33)

56. He trains my hands for battle. (Psalms 18:34)

57. The Lord gives me his shield of victory, and His right hand sustains me; He stoops down to make me great. (Psalms 18:35)

58. The Lord is my shepherd I shall not be in want. (Psalms 23:1)

59. He makes me lie down in green pastures and leads me beside quiet waters. (Psalms 23:2)

60. He restores my soul. He guides me in paths of righteousness for His name's sake. (Psalms 23:3)

61. Even though I walk through the valley of the shadow of death, I will fear no evil, for God is with me; His rod and his staff comfort me. (Psalms 23:4)

62. He prepares a table before me in the presence of my enemies. He anoints my head with oil; my cup overflows. (Psalms 23:5)

63. Surely goodness and love will follow me all the days of my life, and I will dwell in the house of the Lord forever. (Psalms 23:6)

64. The earth is the Lord's and everything in it, the world, and all who live in it. (Psalms 24:1)

65. He founded it upon the seas and established it upon the waters. (Psalms 24:2)

66. I will receive blessing from the Lord and vindication from God my Savior. (Psalms 24:5)

67. The Lord will show me His ways and teach me his paths. (Psalms 25:4)

68. He will guide me into all truth and touch me. (Psalms 25:5)

69. The Lord will vindicate me, for I have led a blameless life; I have trusted in the Lord without wavering. (Psalms 26:1)

70. Test me, O Lord, and try me, examine my heart and my mind. (Psalms 26:2)

71. God's love is ever before me, and I walk continually in his truth. (Psalms 26:3)

72. I love the house where God lives, the place where his glory dwells. (Psalms 26:8)

73. The Lord is my light and my salvation-whom shall, I fear? The Lord is the stronghold of my life-of whom shall I be afraid? (Psalms 27:1)

74. One thing I ask of the Lord, this is what I seek: That I may dwell in the house of Lord all the days of my life, to gaze upon the beauty of the Lord and to seek Him in His temple. (Psalms 27:4)

75. In the day of trouble God will keep me safe in his dwelling: He will hide me in the shelter of his tabernacle and set me high upon a rock. (Psalms 27:5)

76. I will sing and make music to the Lord. (Psalms 27:6)

77. As a righteous man I may have many troubles, but the Lord will deliver me from them all. (Psalms 34:19)

78. God will protect all my bones, not one of them will be broken. (Psalms 34:20)

79. I was young and now I am old, yet I have never seen the righteous forsaken or their children begging bread. (Psalms 37:25)

80. I will always be generous and lend freely; My children will be blessed. (Psalms 37:26)

81. I will wait for the Lord and keep His way. He will exalt me to inherit the land: The wicked are cut off, and I will see it. (Psalms 37:36)

82. I am poor and needy; And the Lord is thinking of me. He is my helper and my deliverer; My God, will not delay. (Psalms 40:17)

83. I am blessed because I have regard for the weak; The Lord delivers me in times of trouble. (Psalms 41:1)

84. The Lord will protect me and preserve my life; He will bless me in the land and not surrender me to the desire of my foes. (Psalms 41:2)

85. Create in me a pure heart, O God, and renew a steadfast spirit within me. (Psalms 51:10)

86. Restore to me the joy of your salvation and grant me a willing spirit, to sustain me. (Psalms 51:12)

87. God will not despise my broken spirit and my broken and contrite heart. (Psalms 51:17)

88. I will shout to the Lord with gladness; and come before Him with joyful songs. (Psalms 100:1-2)

89. I know that the Lord is God. It is He who made us, and I am His. I am part of His people, the sheep of His pasture. (Psalms 100:3)

90. The Lord is good, and his love endures forever; His faithfulness continues through all generations. (Psalms 100:5)

91. I am at rest once more. The Lord has been good to my soul. (Psalms 116:7)

92. The Lord has delivered my soul from death, my eyes from tears, and my feet from stumbling. (Psalms 116:8)

93. As a young man I can keep myself pure by living according to God's word. (Psalms 119:9)

94. I have hidden your word in my heart that I might not sin against you. (Psalms 119:11)

95. Praise be to you, O Lord, Teach me your decrees. With my lips I recount all the laws that come from your mouth. (Psalms 119:13)

96. Your word is a lamp to my feet and a light to my path. (Psalms 119:105)

97. My help comes from the Lord, the maker of heaven and earth. (Psalms 121:2)

98. My sons are a heritage from the Lord, children a reward from Him. (Psalms 127:3)

99. I will trust in the Lord with all my heart and lean not on my own understanding; in all my ways I will acknowledge Him, and He will make my paths straight. (Proverbs 3:5,6)

100. The fear of the Lord is the beginning of my wisdom, and knowledge of the Holy One is my understanding. (Proverbs 9:10)

101. I have found a wife, and this is good because now I will receive favor from the Lord. (Proverbs 18:22)

102. When I am kind to the poor I lend to the Lord, and He will reward me for what I have done. (Proverbs 19:17)

103. When my ways seem right, the Lord weighs my heart. (Proverbs 21:2)

104. I will train up a child in the way he should go, and when he is old, he will not turn from it. (Proverbs 22:6)

105. I will come and reason with the Lord. "Though my sins are like scarlet, they shall be as white as snow. Though they are red as crimson, they shall be like wool." (Isaiah 1:18)

106. Then I heard the voices of the Lord saying, "Whom

shall I send? And who will go for us?" and I said, "Here I am send me!" (Isaiah 6:8)

107. God will keep my mind in perfect peace because my mind is steadfast, and it trusts in Him. (Isaiah 26:3)

108. I will trust in the Lord forever, for the Lord, the Lord, is the rock eternal. (Isaiah 26:3)

109. God is saying to me right now, "This is the way, walk in it." (Isaiah 30:21)

110. God has declared the plans He has for me, plans to prosper me and not harm me, plans to give me hope and a future. (Jeremiah 29:11)

111. He was pierced for my transgressions, crushed for my iniquities; the punishment that brought me peace was upon Him, and by his wounds I am healed. (Isaiah 53:5)

112. When I hope in the Lord, I will renew my strength. I will soar on wings like eagles; I will run and not grow weary; I will walk and not faint. (Isaiah 40:31)

113. I will not fear for God has redeemed me; He has summoned me by name. (Isaiah 43:1)

114. When I pass through the waters, He will be with me; and when I pass through the rivers, they will not sweep over me. When I walk through the fire, I will not be burned; the flames will not set me ablaze. (Isaiah 43:2)

115. I will forget the former things; and not dwell in the past. (Isaiah 43:18)

116. God is doing a new thing in me and it's springing up ... He is making a way in the desert and streams in the wasteland. (Isaiah 43:19)

117. He will give me treasures of darkness, riches stored in secret places, so that I may know that He is the Lord. (Isaiah 45:3)

118. God is God, and there is no other; there is none like him. (Isaiah 46:9)

119. He makes known the end from the beginning. (Isaiah 46:10)

120. I will enlarge the place of my tent; I will stretch the tent curtains wide; I will not hold back; I will lengthen the cords and strengthen the stakes. (Isaiah 54:2)

121. No weapon forged against me will prevail. (Isaiah 54:17)

122. I will share my food with the hungry, provide the poor wanderer with shelter; when I see the naked, I will clothe him and will not turn away. (Isaiah 58:7)

123. The Lord will give me a new heart and put a new spirit in me; He will remove the heart of stone and give me a heart of flesh. (Ezekiel 36:2)

124. I will write down the revelation and make it plain on tablets. (Habakkuk 2:2)

125. I will listen to advice and accept discipline so that I would be counted among the wise. (Proverbs 19:20)

126. I will bring the whole tithe into the storehouse that there may be food in my house. (Malachi 3:10)

127. God will throw open the floodgates of heaven and pour out so much blessing that I will not have room enough for it. (Malachi 3:10)

128. God will prevent pests from devouring my crops and the vines in my fields will not cast their fruit. (Malachi 3:11)

129. "All the nations will call me blessed, for it will be a delightful land." Says the Lord Almighty. (Malachi 3:12)

130. "I am His," says the Lord Almighty, "I am His treasured possession." (Malachi 3:17)

131. The Lord is sending the prophet Elijah and He will turn the hearts of the fathers to their children and the hearts of children to their fathers. (Malachi 4:5-6)

132. I will ask the Lord and He will make the nations my inheritance, the ends of the earth my possession. (Psalms 2:8)

133. Lord I will trust in your unfailing love; my heart rejoices in your salvation. (Psalms 13:5)

134. You have heard my cry for mercy as I call to you for help, I will lift up my hands toward your Most Holy Place. (Psalms 28:2)

135. I trust in you, O Lord; I say, "you are God." My times are in your hands. (Psalms 31:14-15)

136. I know the angel of the Lord is encamping around me because I fear him, and he will deliver me. (Psalms 34:7)

137. I will keep my tongue from evil and my lips from speaking lies. (Psalms 34:13)

138. I will delight myself in the Lord and he will give me the desires of my heart. (Psalms 37:4)

139. I will be still and know that He is God. (Psalms 46:10)

140. I will trust in the Lord with all my heart and not lean in my own understanding. (Proverbs 3:5)

141. In all my ways I will submit to him and he will make my paths straight. (Proverbs 3:6)

142. I will not withhold good to those who deserve it when it is in my power to act. (Proverbs 3:27)

143. I know my days will be many, and years will be added to my life. (Proverbs 9:11)

144. As righteous my fruit is a tree of life, and as I win souls, I am wise. (Proverbs 11:30)

145. I will gather money little by little to make it grow. (Proverbs 13:11)

146. I will heed discipline and correction to avoid poverty and shame and be honored. (Proverbs 13:18)

147. I will honor God by being kind to the needy. (Proverbs 14:31)

148. I will plan my course, but I will let the Lord determine my steps. (Proverbs 16:9)

149. I choose a cheerful heart for it is good medicine for me. (Proverbs 17:22)

150. Iron sharpens iron, I will choose to sharpen another. (Proverbs 27:17)

151. I will bring my whole tithe into God's storehouse, that there may be food in my house, God will then throw open the flood gates of Heaven and pour out so much blessing to me that there will not be enough room to store it. (Malachi 3:10)

NEW TESTAMENT SCRIPTURES

1. I will be a voice calling out, to prepare the way of the Lord and make straight paths for Him. (Matthew 3:3)

2. I will not live on bread alone, but on every word that comes from the mouth of God. (Matthew 4:4)

3. "Away from me, Satan! For it is written I will

worship the Lord my God and serve Him only." (Matthew 4:10)

4. I will follow Jesus because He said He will make me a fisher of men. (Matthew 4:14)

5. I will hunger and thirst for righteousness, because then I will be filled. (Matthew 5:6)

6. I will be merciful, so that I will be shown mercy. (Matthew 5:7)

7. I will be of a pure heart so that I can see God. (Matthew 5:8)

8. I will be a peacemaker, so that I would be called a son of God. (Matthew 5:9)

9. If I am persecuted because of righteousness, I know then that the Kingdom of Heaven is mine. (Matthew 5:10)

10. I am the salt of the earth. (Matthew 5:13)

11. I am the light of the world. (Matthew 5: 14)

12. My Father in Heaven, I hallow your name, may your kingdom come, may your will be done in my life on earth as it is in heaven. Lord, give me this day my daily bread, forgive me Lord for my debts as I forgive my debtors. Lord, lead me not into temptation but deliver me from evil, for yours is the kingdom, the power, and the glory, forever, Amen! (Matthew 6:9-13)

13. I will store up for myself treasures in heaven, where moth and rust do not destroy, and where thieves do not break in and steal. (Matthew 6:20)

14. If I worry, I cannot add a single hour to my life. (Matthew 6:27)

15. I will seek first his Kingdom and all his Righteousness, then I know that all these things will be given to me. (Matthew 6:33)

16. I will ask and it will be given to me; I will seek, and I will find; I will knock and the door will be opened to me. (Matthew 7:7)

17. Wide is the gate that leads to Destruction, and many enter through it, but small is the gate and narrow the road that leads to life and only a few find it. I choose the narrow gate. (Matthew 7:13-14)

18. By their fruit I will recognize the true followers of Christ. (Matthew 7:20)

19. I will do the will of my father so that I can enter the Kingdom of Heaven. (Matthew 7:21)

20. I will build my Spiritual house on the rock, who is Jesus! (Matthew 7:24)

21. The harvest is plentiful, but the workers are few. I will ask the Lord of the Harvest, to send workers into his harvest field. (Matthew 9:37-38)

22. I will Preach this message: "The Kingdom of Heaven

is near, I will heal the sick, raise the dead and drive out demons. (Matthew 10:7-8)

23. I will not be worried about what to say, or how to say it. At that time, I will be given what to say, for it will not be me speaking, but the spirit of my Father speaking through me. (Matthew 10:19-20)

24. From the days of John the Baptist until now, the Kingdom of Heaven has been forcefully advancing, and forceful men lay hold of it. I will be one of them. (Matthew 11:12)

25. I will come to him, because I am weary and burdened, and I know He will give me rest. (Matthew 11:28)

26. I will take his yoke upon me and learn of Him, for I know He is gentle and humble in heart, and I will find rest for my soul. (Matthew 11:29)

27. His yoke is easy, and his burden is light. (Matthew 11:30)

28. I will pray in His name, so that the nations will put their hope in Him. (Matthew 12:21)

29. Out of the abundance of my heart my mouth speaks. (Matthew 12:34)

30. I will be the one who receives the seed that has fallen on good soil, I will be the one who hears the word of God and understands it. I will produce a

crop, yielding a hundred, sixty or thirty times what was sown. (Matthew 13:23)

31. I will honor God with my lips, and my heart will be near to him. (Matthew 15:8)

32. You are the Christ, the son of the living God. (Matthew 16:16)

33. I am _____ and upon this rock Jesus will build His church, and the gates of Hell will not prevail against it. (Matthew 16:18)

34. I have been given the keys of the Kingdom of Heaven, and whatever I bind on earth will be bound in heaven, and whatever I loose on earth will be loosed in heaven. (Matthew 16:19)

35. I will come after Christ; I will deny myself and take up my cross and follow him. (Matthew 16:24)

36. I will say unto this mountain move, and it will move. Nothing will be impossible for me. (Matthew 17:20)

37. I will have childlike faith so that I may enter the Kingdom of Heaven. (Matthew 18:3)

38. I will leave the ninety-nine and go look for the one sheep that wandered off. (Matthew 18:12)

39. I know that if two of us on earth agree about anything I ask for; it will be done for me by my father in heaven. (Matthew 18:19)

40. I know that where two or three come together in Jesus name, Jesus will be with them. (Matthew 18:20)

41. I will forgive my brother when he sins against me. (Matthew 18:21)

42. I will not murder, I will not commit adultery, I will not steal, I will not give false testimony, I will honor my father and mother, and love my neighbor as myself. (Matthew 19:18-19)

43. I will give to the poor to have treasure in heaven, and I will follow him. (Matthew 19:21)

44. With man it is impossible, but with God all things are possible. (Matthew 19:26)

45. Lord I know that you did not come to be served, but to serve, and to give your life as a ransom for many. (Matthew 20:28)

46. Lord your house will be called a House of Prayer. (Matthew 21:13

47. I will believe, and I will receive whatever I ask for in prayer. (Matthew 21:22

48. Lord I know that you are the God of Abraham, The God of Isaac, and the God of Jacob, you are not the God of the dead but of the living. (Matthew 22:32)

49. I will love the Lord my God with all my heart, and with all my soul, and with all my mind. (Matthew 22:37)

50. I will love my neighbor as myself. (Matthew 22:39)

51. "Blessed is he who comes in the name of the Lord." (Matthew 23:39)

52. I will stand firm to the end and be saved. (Matthew 24:13)

53. I know that this gospel of the Kingdom must be preached to all the world as a testimony to all nations, and then the end will come. (Matthew 24:14)

54. I know that heaven and earth will pass away, but God's word will never pass away. (Matthew 24:35)

55. I will keep watch for Jesus return because I don't know what day the Lord will come. (Matthew 24:42)

56. As his servant I will always be doing good, so when my master comes, He will find me doing good. (Matthew 24:46)

57. I know that in the future I will see the son of God sitting at the right hand of the Mighty One and coming on the clouds of heaven. (Matthew 26:64)

58. All authority in heaven and on earth has been given to Jesus. I am to go and make disciples of all nations, baptizing them in the name of the Father and of the Son and of the Holy spirit, I am to teach them to obey everything Jesus has commanded me, knowing

that Jesus is with me always, to the very end of the age. (Matthew 28:18-20)

59. I will prepare the way for the Lord and make his paths straight. (Mark 1:3)

60. I know that the time has now come; the Kingdom of God is near. I will preach repentance and believe the good news. (Mark 1:15)

61. "I am willing", Jesus said "be clean!" (Mark 1:41)

62. It is not the healthy who need a doctor, but the sick. He has not come to call the righteous, but sinners. (Mark 2:17)

63. Whoever does God's will be my brother and sister and mother. (Mark 3:34)

64. If I just touch his clothes, I will be healed. (Mark 5:28)

65. The Lord is sending me out and giving me authority over evil spirits. (Mark 6:7)

66. I will go out to preach so that people should repent. (Mark 6:12)

67. I will meditate on this that what comes out of man is what makes him unclean. "For from within, men's hearts come evil thoughts, sexual immorality, theft, murder, adultery greed, malice, deceit, lewdness, envy, slander, arrogance and folly. All these evils

come from inside and make a man unclean. I will abstain from these." (Mark 7:20-23)

68. I will come after him, I will deny myself and take up my cross and follow him. (Mark 8:34)

69. I will not be ashamed of the Lord's words in this adulterous and sinful generation, because if I do Jesus will be ashamed of me when He comes in His Father's glory with the holy angels. (Mark 8:38)

70. Everything is possible if I believe. (Mark 9:23)

71. Lord I do believe; help me overcome my unbelief. (Mark 9:24)

72. If I welcome a little child in His name, He will welcome me. (Mark 9:37)

73. In my marriage I am no longer two but one flesh. Therefore, what God has joined together, let man not separate. (Mark 10:8-9)

74. I will let the children come to Jesus, and not hinder them, for the Kingdom of God belongs to them. (Mark 10:14)

75. I will follow the commandments of the Lord: I will not murder, I will not commit adultery, I will not steal, I will not give false testimony, I will not defraud anybody, I will honor my father and mother. (Mark 10:19)

76. With man it is impossible, but not "with God; All things are possible with God." (Mark 10:27)

77. I will become a servant of all and not Lord it over others, then God would acknowledge me as great. (Mark 10:42-44)

78. Jesus came not to be served, but to serve, and to give his life as a ransom for many. (Mark10:45)

79. "Hosanna! Blessed is he who comes in the name of the Lord." (Mark 11:9)

80. "God's House will be called a House of Prayer for all nations." (Mark 11:17)

81. "I will have faith in God." (Mark 11:22)

82. I will say to this mountain, go throw yourself in the sea. And I will not doubt in my heart, but I will believe that what I have said will happen. (Mark 11:23)

83. Whatever I ask in prayer, I will believe that I have received it. (Mark 11:24)

84. When I stand praying if I hold anything against anyone, I will forgive him, so that my Father in heaven may forgive my sins. (Mark 11:25)

85. I will give to Caesar what is Caesar's and to God what is God's. (Mark 12:17)

86. Jesus is not the God of the dead, but of the living. (Mark 12:27)

87. I will not worry about what I am to say. But I will say whatever is given to me at the time, for it will not be me speaking, but the Holy Spirit. (Mark 13:11)

88. I will watch and pray so that I will not fall into temptation. My spirit is willing, but my body is weak. (Mark 14:38)

89. I know that I will see the son of man sitting at the right hand of the mighty one and coming on the clouds of heaven. (Mark 14:62)

90. I now can enter, because the curtain of the temple was torn in two from top to bottom. (Mark 15:38)

91. Jesus is saying to me to "Go into all the world and preach the good news to all creation, whoever believes and is baptized will be saved, but whoever does not believe will be condemned. (Mark 16:15-16)

92. I know that signs will accompany me when I believe: In His name I will drive out demons; I will pick up snakes with my hands; And if I drink deadly poison, it will not hurt me at all; And I know that when I place my hands on the sick people, they will get well. (Mark 16:17-18)

93. Jesus was taken up and is now sitting at the right hand of God. (Mark 16:19)

94. "The Lord has done this for me," He has shown favor and taken away my disgrace among the people. (Luke 1:25)

95. "Glory to God in the highest, and on earth peace to men on whom his favor rest." (Luke 2:14)

96. I am a voice calling in the desert, prepare the way for the Lord, make straight paths for Him. (Luke 3:4)

97. I will not put the Lord my God to the test. (Luke 4:12)

98. The spirit of the Lord is on me, because he has anointed me to preach good news to the poor. He has sent me to proclaim freedom for the prisoners and recovery of sight for the blind, to release the oppressed, to proclaim the year of the Lord's favor. (Luke 3:18-19)

99. I will love my enemies and do good to those who hate me, I will bless those who curse me and pray for those who mistreat me. (Luke 6:27-28)

100. I will give to everyone who asks me, and if anyone takes what belongs to me, I will not demand it back. I will do to others as I would have them do to me. (Luke 6:30-31)

101. I will give and it will be given to me. A good measure, pressed down, shaken together and running over, will be poured into my lap, for with the measure I use it will be measured back to me. (Luke 6:38)

102. I will hear God's word and put it into practice. (Luke 6:49)

103. I am blessed because I will not fall away on account of Jesus. (Luke 7:23)

104. I will prepare the way before Jesus comes. (Luke 7:27)

105. My faith has saved me. I can now go in peace. (Luke 7:50)

106. The knowledge of the secrets of the Kingdom of God has been given to me. (Luke 8:10)

107. I will not be afraid. I will just believe, and I will be healed. (Luke 8:50)

108. What would profit me to gain the whole world and lose my soul. (Luke 9:25)

109. I will not be ashamed of Jesus and His words, in that way Jesus will not be ashamed of me when he comes in His glory. (Luke 9:26)

110. I will let the dead bury their own dead, and I will go and proclaim the Kingdom of God. (Luke 9:60)

111. I will put my hand to the plow and never look back so I can be fit for the Lord's service. (Luke 9:62)

112. I have been given authority to trample on snakes and scorpions and to overcome all the power of the

enemy and I know that nothing will harm me. (Luke 10:19)

113. I am blessed because I hear the word of God and I obey it. (Luke 11:28)

114. I know the truth and I will see the Kingdom of God because I am born again. (John 3:3)

115. I will lift up Jesus just like Moses lifted up the serpent in the desert. (John 3:14)

116. He must become greater and I must become less. (John 3:30)

117. Because I believe in the son, I have eternal life. (John 3:36)

118. I will drink the water that Jesus gives me to drink so that I will never thirst. This water will become in me a spring of water welling up to eternal life. (John 4:14)

119. I will worship the Father in spirit and in truth, for this is the kind of worshiper the father seeks. (John 4:24)

120. My food is to do the will of He who sent me and to finish His work. (John 4:34)

121. I will hear His word and believe Him so that I can inherit eternal life and cross over from death to life. (John 5:24)

122. I will not work for food that spoils but for food that endures to eternal life. (John 6:27)

123. Jesus is the bread of life; I will go to him and know I will never go hungry or thirsty. (John 6:35)

124. I will cling to the words God has spoken because they are spirit and they are life. (John 6:63)

125. I will believe in Him and streams of living waters will flow from within me. (John 7:38)

126. Jesus said to me "neither do I condemn you," Go now and leave your life of sin. (John 8:11)

127. When I follow Jesus, I will never be in darkness, but I will have the light of life. (John 8:12)

128. I will know the truth, and the truth will set me free. (John 8:32)

129. The devil was a murderer from the beginning, not holding the truth, for there is no truth in him. When he lies, he speaks his native language, for he is a liar and the father of lies. (John 8:44)

130. I will keep his word, and I will never see death. (John 8:51)

131. Jesus came to give me life and have it to the full. And I know the devil came to steal, to kill and destroy. (John 10:10)

132. He is the Good Shepherd and I am his sheep and I know him. (John 10:14)

133. Jesus has given me eternal life and I will never perish: No one will snatch me out of his hand. (John 10:28)

134. Jesus is the resurrection and the life. Because I believe in Him, I will live and will never die. (John 11:25)

135. Jesus wept. (John 11:35)

136. Jesus said the poor will always be with us. (John 12:8)

137. When I lift Jesus up from the earth, He will draw all men to himself. (John 12:32)

138. A new command he has given me: to love one another as He has loved me. (John 13:34)

139. I know that all men will know that we are his disciples by the love they have for one another. (John 13:35)

140. I will not let my heart be troubled. I will trust in God. (John 14:1)

141. .In my Father's house are many rooms and Jesus went there to prepare a place for me. (John 14:2)

142. Jesus is the way the truth and the life and no one comes to the Father but through Him. (John 14:6)

143. Greater works will I do because Jesus went to the Father. (John 14:12)

144. If I ask anything in His name, He will do it. (John 14:14)

145. When I love him I will obey his teachings. Then my Father will come and make my home with him. (John 14:23)

146. The Holy Spirit will teach me all things and will remind me of everything He has said to me. (John 14:26)

147. I will not allow my heart to be troubled and I will not be afraid. When I do this God will give me peace not like the world gives. (John 14:27)

148. Jesus is the true vine and the Father the gardener. (John 15:1)

149. I am clean by the word God spoke to me. (John 15:3)

150. If I remain in Him, He will remain in me. (John 15:4)

151. I cannot bear fruit without him. (John 15:5)

152. I will remain in his love so that his joy in me would be complete. (John 15:11)

153. Greater love has no one than this, that He lay down His life for me, His friend. (John 15:13)

154. When He, the spirit of truth, comes, He will guide me into all truth... (John 16:13)

155. I will ask and I will receive so that my Joy may be complete. (John 16:24)

156. In this world I will have trouble, but I will take heart because He has overcome the world. (John 16:33)

157. Jesus prayed for me to be one with Him. (John 17:21)

158. Blessed am I who has not seen but believes. (John 20:29)

159. I will receive power when the Holy Spirit comes upon me; and I will be a witness in Jerusalem, and in all Judea and Samaria, and to the ends of the earth. (Acts 1:8)

160. I will devote myself to the apostles teaching and to the fellowship, to the breaking of bread and to prayer. (Acts 2:42)

161. I will repent; Then turn to God, so that my sins may be wiped out, then times of refreshing will come from the Lord. (Acts 3:19)

162. Salvation is found in no one else, for there is no other name under heaven given to men by which we must be saved. (Acts 4:12)

163. Lord, stretch out your hand and heal and perform miraculous signs and wonders through the name of your Holy servant Jesus. (Acts 4:30)

164. I am not ashamed of the gospel, because it is the

power of God for the salvation of everyone who believes. (Romans 1:16)

165. I know that all have sinned and fallen short of the glory of God. (Romans 3:23)

166. I am a blessed man, because God has forgiven me, and he will not count my sin against me. (Romans 4:8)

167. By faith I will call those things that are not, as though they were. (Romans 4:17)

168. Jesus was delivered to death for my sins and was raised to life for my Justification. (Romans 4:25)

169. I now have peace with God through our Lord Jesus Christ because of justified faith. (Romans 5:1)

170. I have gained access by faith into his grace. (Romans 5:2)

171. I rejoice in my sufferings, because I know my sufferings produce perseverance and character, and character produces hope. (Romans 5:4)

172. God demonstrated his love for me, that while I was still a sinner, Christ died for me. (Romans 5:8)

173. I have died to sin and I will not live in it any longer. (Romans 6:1)

174. I am now dead to sin and alive to God in Christ Jesus. (Romans 6:11)

175. I will not allow sin to reign in my mortal body so that I obey its evil desires. (Romans 6:12)

176. I will offer myself to God who has brought me from death to life, and I offer all the parts of my body to Him as instruments of righteousness. (Romans 6:13)

177. Sin will not be my master, because I am not under law, but under grace. (Romans 6:14)

178. My obedience to God will lead to righteousness. (Romans 6:16)

179. I have been set free from sin and have become a slave to righteousness. (Romans 6:18)

180. I now feel no condemnation because I am Christ's child. (Romans 8:1)

181. Through Christ Jesus the law of the spirit of life has set me free from the law of sin and death. (Romans 8:2)

182. The wages of sin is death, but I have received the gift of God which is eternal life in Christ Jesus our Lord. (Romans 6:23)

183. My mind is set not on my evil desires but upon what the spirit desires. (Romans 8:5)

184. The mind of sinful man is death, but my mind is controlled by the spirit of life and peace. (Romans 8:6)

185. I have the spirit of Christ; therefore, I belong to

Christ because Christ is in me. My body is dead because of sin. (Romans 8:9)

186. But my spirit is alive because of righteousness. (Romans 8:10)

187. The same spirit that raised Jesus from the dead is living in me. (Romans 8:11)

188. I am led by the spirit of God; Therefore I am one of the sons of God. (Romans 8:14)

189. God's spirit testifies with my spirit that I am His child. (Romans 8:16)

190. As His child I am an heir of God and Christ so we can share in their glory. (Romans 8:17)

191. The spirit of God helps me in my weakness. I don't know what I ought to pray for, but the spirit in me intercedes for me with groans that words cannot express. (Romans 8:26)

192. And I know that all things will work together for my good because I love God and He has called me to His purpose. (Romans 8:28)

193. God is for me, who can be against me. (Romans 8:31)

194. Christ Jesus who died and was raised to life is at the right hand of God interceding for me. (Romans 8:34)

195. Nothing can separate me from the love of God –

no trouble or hardship or persecution of famine or nakedness or danger or sword. (Romans 8:35)

196. In all these things I am more than a conqueror through Him who loved me. (Romans 8:37)

197. For I am convinced that neither death nor life, neither angels nor demons, neither the present nor the future, nor any powers, neither height nor depth, nor anything else in all creation, will be able to separate me from the love of God that is in Christ Jesus my Lord. (Romans 8:38-39)

198. I speak the truth in Christ. I am not lying. My conscience confirms it in the Holy Spirit. (Romans 9:1)

199. God raised me up for this very purpose, that He might display His power in me and so His name might be proclaimed in all the earth. (Romans 9:17)

200. I confess my Lord with my mouth, "Jesus is Lord," and I will believe in my heart that God raised Him from the dead. In this proclamation I know I am saved. (Romans 10:9)

201. I will call on the name of the Lord and be saved. (Romans 10:13)

202. I will offer my body as a living sacrifice, holy and pleasing to God – this is my spiritual act of worship. (Romans 12:1)

203. .I will not conform any longer to the patterns of this world, but I choose to be transformed by renewing my mind. Then I will be able to test and approve what God's will is for me, His good and perfect will. (Romans 12:2)

204. My love will be sincere. I will hate what is evil; cling to what is good. (Romans 12:9)

205. I will be devoted to others with brotherly love. I will honor others above myself. (Romans 12:10)

206. I will keep my spiritual fervor and serve the Lord. (Romans 12:11)

207. I will be joyful in hope, patient in affliction, faithful in prayer. (Romans 12:12)

208. I will practice hospitality by sharing with God's people who are in need. (Romans 12:13)

209. I will bless those who persecute me and bless those who curse me. (Romans 12:14)

210. I will rejoice with those who rejoice; mourn with those who mourn. Live in harmony with everyone. (Romans 12:15-16)

211. I will not repay evil for evil. But I will be careful to do what is right in the eyes of everyone. (Romans 12:17)

212. If it is possible, as far as it depends on me, I will live at peace with everyone. (Romans 12:18)

213. .If my enemy is hungry, I will feed him. If he's thirsty, I will give him something to drink. God said, "It is mine to avenge; I will repay." (Romans 12:19-20)

214. I will not be overcome by evil, but I will overcome evil with good. (Romans 12:21)

215. God has established governing authorities for me. Therefore, I will submit myself to the authorities that exist. (Romans 13:1)

216. As a servant of God, I will give everyone what I owe them, taxes, revenue, then respect, then honor. (Romans 13:6-7)

217. I will put aside the deeds of darkness and put on the armor of light. (Romans 13:12)

218. I will clothe myself with the Lord Jesus Christ, and not think about how to gratify the desires of the sinful nature. (Romans 13:14)

219. I will accept those whose faith is weak, without passing judgment. (Romans 14:1)

220. As I live, I live to the Lord; and if I die, I die to the Lord – so whether I live or die, I belong to the Lord. (Romans. 14:8)

221. I know someday I will give an account of myself to God. (Romans 14:12)

222. For the Kingdom of God is not a matter of eating and drinking, but of righteousness, peace and joy

in the Holy Spirit. As I serve Christ in this way, I will please Him and be approved by men. (Romans 14:17-18)

223. I will make every effort to do what leads to peace and to mutual edification. (Romans 14:19)

224. It has always been my ambition to preach the gospel where Christ was not known, so that I would not be building on someone else's foundation. (Romans 15:20)

225. I know that the God of peace will soon crush Satan under my feet. (Romans 16:20)

226. God has called me into fellowship with his son Jesus Christ our Lord. (1 Corinthians 1:9)

227. When I boast, I will boast in the Lord. (1 Corinthians 1:31)

228. I will bow my knees before Him, my tongue will confess to God. (Romans 14:11)

229. No eye has seen, no ear has heard, no mind has conceived what God has prepared for those who love him. But God has revealed this to me by His spirit. (1 Corinthians 2:9-10)

230. I have the mind of Christ. (1 Corinthians 2:16)

231. When I plant the seed, someone else will water it, but God will make it grow. (1 Corinthians 3:6)

232. I am one of God's fellow workers; because I am God's field, I am God's building. (1 Corinthians 3:9)

233. By the grace God has given me, I laid a foundation as an expert builder. I will be careful how I build it, because Christ Jesus already laid the foundation. (1 Corinthians 3:10-11)

234. I will judge nothing before the appointed time. I will wait till the Lord comes. He will bring to light what has happened in darkness and will expose the motives of men's hearts. (1 Corinthians 4:5)

235. I will not associate myself with anyone who calls himself a brother and is sexually immoral or greedy, an idolater or a slander, a drunkard or a swindler. (1 Corinthians 5:11)

236. My body is the temple of the Holy Spirit, who is in me, whom I have received from God. I am not my own. I was bought with a price. I will honor God with my body. (1 Corinthians 6:19-20)

237. I will run in such a way as to get the prize. The prize is to get a crown that will last forever. (1 Corinthians 9:25)

238. God is faithful. He will not let me be tempted beyond what I can bear. But when I am tempted, He will provide a way out so that I can stand up under it. (1 Corinthians 10:13)

239. Whatever I eat and drink or whatever I do, I will do it for the glory of the Lord. (l Corinthians 10:31)

240. People can follow my example, as I follow the example of Christ. (1 Corinthians 11:1)

241. .The nine gifts of the spirit are: Wisdom, Knowledge, Faith, Healing, Miracles, Prophecy, Discernment, Tongues, and the interpretation of tongues. (1 Corinthians 12:8-11)

242. I will eagerly desire the greater gifts. (1 Corinthians 12:31)

243. My love should be patient and kind; it should not envy or boast. It should not be proud or rude or self-seeking. My love should not easily be angered and should not keep records of wrongs. (1 Corinthians 13:4-5)

244. My love will not delight in evil but will rejoice with the truth. It will always protect, always trust, always hope, and always persevere. (1 Corinthians 13:6-7)

245. Love will never fail me. (1 Corinthians 13:8)

246. There are three things that remain: Faith, Hope and Love. But the greatest of these is love. (1 Corinthians 13:13)

247. I will be eager to prophesy. I will not forbid speaking in tongues. (1 Corinthians 14:39)

248. Christ died for my sins according to the scriptures.

He was buried, and then He was raised on the third day according to the scriptures. (1 Corinthians 15:3-4)

249. I will not be misled. I will not hang around bad company because it corrupts my good character. (1 Corinthians 15:33)

250. I will stand firm and let nothing move me. I will give myself fully to the work of the Lord, because I know that my labor in the Lord is not in vain. (1 Corinthians 15:58)

251. I will be on my guard; I will stand firm in the faith; and be a man of courage and strength. (1 Corinthians 16:13)

252. I will do everything in love. (1 Corinthians 16:14)

253. God comforts me in all my troubles, so that I may comfort those in trouble. (2 Corinthians 1:4)

254. Now it is God who has anointed me to stand firm in Him. (2 Corinthians 1:21)

255. He has set his seal of ownership in me and put his spirit in my heart as a deposit. Guaranteeing what is to come. (2 Corinthians 1:21-22)

256. I have asked forgiveness in the sight of Christ, in order that Satan might not outwit me. For I am not unaware of his schemes. (2 Corinthians 2:10-11)

257. I thank God, who always leads me in a triumphal

procession in Christ and through me. He spreads the fragrance of his knowledge. (2 Corinthians 2:14

258. I am to God the aroma of Christ. (2 Corinthians 2:15)

259. I am a letter written by God for everyone to read. (2 Corinthians 3:2)

260. God has written in me not with ink, but with the spirit of the living God. (2 Corinthians 3:3)

261. The letter kills, but the spirit gives life. (2 Corinthians 3:6)

262. Now the Lord is the spirit, and where the spirit of the Lord is, there is freedom. (2 Corinthians 3:17)

263. God has shined His light in my heart to give me the light of the knowledge of the glory of God in the face of Christ. (2 Corinthians 4:4-6)

264. I have this treasure in a jar of clay to show that this all-surpassing power is from God and not from me. (2 Corinthians 4:7)

265. I am hard pressed on every side, but not crushed; perplexed, but not in despair. (2 Corinthians 4:8)

266. I am persecuted, but not abandoned; struck down, but not destroyed. (2 Corinthians 4:9)

267. I am carrying in my body the death of Jesus, so that the life of Jesus may also be revealed in my body. (2 Corinthians 4:10)

268. I know that the one who raised the Lord Jesus from the dead will also raise me with Jesus and present me into His presence. (2 Corinthians 4:14)

269. Outwardly I am wasting away, yet inwardly I am being renewed day by day. (2 Corinthians 4:16)

270. My light and momentary trouble are achieving for me an eternal glory that far outweighs them all. (2 Corinthians 4:17)

271. So I fix my eyes not on what is seen, but on what is unseen. For what I see is temporary, but what is unseen is eternal. (2 Corinthians 4:18)

272. Now it is God who has made me for this very purpose and has given me the spirit as a deposit, guaranteeing what is to come. (2 Corinthians 5:5)

273. I am always confident and know that as long as I am at home in the body I am away from the Lord. (2 Corinthians 5:6)

274. I live by faith, not by sight. (2 Corinthians 5:7)

275. Christ's love compels me, because I am convinced that one died for all, and therefore all died. (2 Corinthians 5:14)

276. I am a new creation. The old has gone, the new has come. (2 Corinthians 5:17)

277. God gave me the ministry of reconciliation. (2 Corinthians 5:18)

278. I am now one of Christ's ambassadors. (2 Corinthians 5:20)

279. God made Jesus who had no sin to be a sin offering for me, so that in Him I might become the righteousness of God. (2 Corinthians 5:21)

280. Now it's the time of God's favor, now is the day of salvation. (2 Corinthians 6:2)

281. I will not be yoked together with unbelievers. For what do righteousness and wickedness have in common? (2 Corinthians 6:14)

282. I am the temple of the living God. God will live with me and walk with me. He will be my God and I will be his people. (2 Corinthians 6:16)

283. I will come out and be separate. I will touch no unclean thing. I know then that God will receive me. (2 Corinthians 6:17)

284. I will purify myself from everything that contaminates my body and my spirit, perfecting holiness out of reverence for God. (2 Corinthians 7:1)

285. Godly sorrow will bring my repentance which leads to my salvation. (2 Corinthians 7:10)

286. I will excel in everything – in faith, in speech, in knowledge, in complete earnestness, in love and in the grace of giving. (2 Corinthians 8:7)

287. When I give, I will give as my heart leads, for God loves a cheerful giver. (2 Corinthians 8:7)

288. For though I live in the world, I do not wage war as the world does. The weapons I fight with are not the weapons of the world. On the contrary, they have divine power to demolish strongholds. (2 Corinthians 10:3-4)

289. I will demolish arguments and every pretension that will set itself up against the knowledge of God, and I take captive every thought to make it obedient to Christ. (2 Corinthians 10:5)

290. When I am weak, then I am strong. His grace is sufficient for me, for His power is made perfect in my weakness. (2 Corinthians 12:9-10)

291. In the sight of God everything I do is for others strengthening. (2 Corinthians 12:19)

292. Likewise, when I am weak in Him yet by God's power, I will live with Him to serve others. (2 Corinthians 13:3)

293. God has given me authority for the building up of others, not the tearing down. (2 Corinthians 13:10)

294. I will aim for perfection, to live in peace and be of one mind. (2 Corinthians 13:11)

295. I have been crucified with Christ and I no longer live, but Christ lives in me. The life I live in the

body, I live by faith in the Son of God who loved me and gave Himself for me. (Galatians 2:20)

296. Because God has declared me righteous, I will live by faith. (Galatians 3:11)

297. I belong to Christ; therefore, I am Abraham's seed, and an heir according to the promise. (Galatians 3:29)

298. I will live in the spirit and not gratify the desires of my sinful nature. (Galatians 5:16)

299. When I am led by the spirit I will not be under the law. (Galatians 5:18)

300. I will live by the fruits of the spirit which are: Love, Joy, Peace, Patience, Kindness, Goodness, Faithfulness, Gentleness, and Self Control. (Galatians 5:22-23)

301. I will sow to please the spirit; from the spirit I will reap eternal life. (Galatians 6:8)

302. I will not become weary in well doing, for at the proper time I will reap a harvest if I don't give up. (Galatians 6:9)

303. God chose me before the creation of the world to be holy and blameless in his sight. (Ephesians 1:4)

304. In love He predestined me and adopted me as His son through Jesus Christ, in accordance with His pleasure and will. (Ephesians 1:5)

305. In Him I have redemption through His blood, the

forgiveness of my sins in accordance with the riches of God's grace that He lavishes on me with all wisdom and understanding. (Ephesians 1:7-8)

306. God has made known to me the mystery of His will according to His good pleasure which is purposed in Christ. (Ephesians 1:9)

307. Having believed, I was marked in Him with a seal, the promised Holy Spirit. (Ephesians 1:13)

308. I am God's possession; the Holy Spirit has been deposited in me as a guarantee of my inheritance until my redemption to the praise of his glory. (Ephesians 1:14)

309. .I was once far away, but I have been brought near in Christ Jesus through His blood. (Ephesians 2:13)

310. Through Jesus Christ, I now have access to the Father by one spirit. (Ephesians 2:18)

311. I am no longer a foreigner or an alien. I am now a fellow citizen with God's people and a member of God's household. (Ephesians 2:19)

312. I am built on the foundation of the apostles and prophets, with Christ Jesus Himself as the chief cornerstone. (Ephesians 2:20)

313. In Him I have been built together to become a dwelling in which God lives by his spirit. (Ephesians 2:22)

314. In Him and through faith in Him I may approach God with freedom and confidence. (Ephesians 3:12)

315. Christ dwells in my heart through faith. I am rooted and established in love. (Ephesians 3:17)

316. I have the power, together with all the saints, to grasp how wide and long and high and deep is the love of Christ. (Ephesians 3:18)

317. I am filled with the measure of all the fullness of God because of His love that surpasses knowledge. (Ephesians 3:19)

318. He is able to do immeasurably more than I ask or imagine, according to His power that is at work within me. (Ephesians 3:20)

319. I choose to live a life worthy of the calling I have received. (Ephesians 4:1)

320. I will be completely humble, gentle, patient and bearing with others in love. (Ephesians 4:2)

321. I will make every effort to keep the unity of the spirit through the bond of peace. (Ephesians 4:3)

322. There is but one Lord, one faith, one baptism; one God and Father of all, who is over all and trough all and in all. (Ephesians 4:5-6)

323. It was He who gave some to be apostles, some to be prophets, some to be evangelists, and some to be pastors and teachers. (Ephesians 4:11)

324. I will no longer be an infant, tossed back and forth by the waves, and blown here and there by every wind of teaching and by the cunning and craftiness of men in their deceitful scheming. (Ephesians 4:14)

325. Instead, I will speak the truth in love, then in all things I will grow into Him who is the head, that is Christ. (Ephesians 4:15)

326. I was taught, with regard to my former way of life, to put off my old self which is being corrupted by its deceitful desires. (Ephesians 4:22)

327. I am to be made new in the attitude of my mind; to put on the new self, created to be like God in true righteousness and holiness. (Ephesians 4:23-24)

328. I will put off falsehood and speak truthfully to my neighbor, for I am a member of His body. (Ephesians 4:25)

329. In my anger I will not sin; I will not let the sun go down while I am still angry. (Ephesians 4:26)

330. I will not give the devil a foothold. (Ephesians 4:27)

331. I will steal no longer, but I will work; doing something useful with my own hands, that I may have something to share with those in need. (Ephesians 4:28)

332. I will not grieve the Holy Spirit of God, with whom

I was sealed for the day of redemption. (Ephesians 4:30)

333. I will get rid of all bitterness, rage and anger, brawling and slander, along with every form of malice. (Ephesians 4:31)

334. I will be kind and compassionate with others, forgiving others, just as Christ forgave me. (Ephesians 4:32)

335. I will live a life of love, just as Christ loved me and gave Himself for me as a fragrant offering and sacrifice to God. (Ephesians 5:2)

336. I will be very careful, then, to live not as unwise but as wise. (Ephesians 5:15)

337. I will make the most of every opportunity because the days are evil. (Ephesians 5:16)

338. I will not be drunk on wine, which leads to debauchery. Instead, I will be filled with the spirit. (Ephesians 5:18)

339. I will speak to others with psalms, hymns and spiritual songs, making music in my heart to the Lord. (Ephesians 5:19)

340. I will always give thanks to God the Father for everything, in the name of our Lord Jesus Christ. (Ephesians 5:20)

341. I will submit to others out of reverence for Christ. (Ephesians 5:21)

342. Christ loved the church so much that he gave Himself up for her to make her holy, cleansing her by the washing with water through the word, and to present her to himself as a radiant church, without stain or wrinkle or any other blemish, but holy and blameless. (Ephesians 5:25-27)

343. I will honor my father and mother which is the first commandment with a promise that it may go well with me and that I may enjoy long life on the earth. (Ephesians 6:2-3)

344. I will be strong in the Lord with His mighty power. (Ephesians 6:10)

345. I will put on the full armor of God so that I can take my stand against the Devil's schemes. (Ephesians 6:11)

346. For I know that my struggle is not against flesh and blood, but against the rulers, against the authorities, against the powers of this dark world and against the spiritual forces of evil in the heavenly realms. (Ephesians 6:12)

347. I will stand firm, with the belt of truth buckled around my waist, with the breastplate of righteousness in place. (Ephesians 6:14)

348. My feet will be fitted with the readiness that comes from the Gospel of peace. (Ephesians 6:15)

349. I will take up the shield of faith, with which I will be able to extinguish all the flaming arrows of the evil one. (Ephesians 6:16)

350. I will put on the helmet of salvation and the sword of the spirit, which is the word of God. (Ephesians 6:17)

351. I will pray in the spirit on all occasions with all kinds of prayers and requests. With this in mind I will be alert and always keep on praying for all the saints. (Ephesians 6:18)

352. I am confident of this, that He who began a good work in me will carry it on to completion until the day of Christ Jesus. (Philippians 1:6)

353. For to me, to live is Christ and to die is gain. (Philippians 1:21)

354. For it has been granted to me on behalf of Christ not only to believe in Him, but also to suffer for Him. (Philippians 1:29)

355. I will do nothing out of selfish ambition or vain conceit, but in humility I will consider others better than myself. (Philippians 2:3)

356. I will not look only on my own interests, but also to the interests of others. (Philippians 2:4)

357. My attitude must be the same as Christ Jesus. (Philippians 2:5)

358. Jesus is the name above every name. (Philippians 2:9)

359. I will therefore work out my own salvation with fear and trembling. (Philippians 2:12)

360. For it is God who works in me to will and act according to his good purpose. (Philippians 2:13)

361. I will do everything without complaining and arguing, so that I may become blameless and pure. A child of God without fault in a crooked and depraved generation. (Philippians 2:14-15)

362. Whatever in my life was to my profit I now consider loss for the sake of Christ. (Philippians 3:7)

363. I consider everything a loss compared to the surpassing greatness of knowing Christ Jesus my Lord. (Philippians 3:8)

364. I want to know Christ and the power of his resurrection and the fellowship of sharing in His sufferings. (Philippians 3:10)

365. I press on to take hold of that for which Christ Jesus took hold of me. (Philippians 3:12)

366. I do not consider myself yet to have taken hold of it. But one thing I do: forgetting what is behind and straining toward what is ahead. (Philippians 3:13)

367. I press on toward the goal to win the prize for which

God has called me heavenward in Christ Jesus. (Philippians 3:14)

368. My citizenship is in Heaven. And I am eagerly awaiting a Savior from there, The Lord Jesus Christ. (Philippians 3:20)

369. I will rejoice in the Lord always. I will say it again: Rejoice! (Philippians 4:4)

370. I will not be anxious about anything, but in everything, by prayer and petition, with thanksgiving, I will present my requests to God. (Philippians 4:6)

371. The peace of God, which will transcend my understanding, will guard my heart and mind in Christ Jesus. (Philippians 4:7)

372. Whatever is true, whatever is noble, whatever is right, whatever is pure, whatever is lovely, whatever is admirable – if anything is excellent or praise worthy – I will think about such things. (Philippians 4:8)

373. Whatever I have learned or received or heard from Him, I will put it into practice. And the God of peace will be with me. (Philippians 4:9)

374. I have learned to be content whatever the circumstances. (Philippians 4:11)

375. I know what it is to be in need, and I know what it

is to have plenty. I have learned the secret of being content in any and every situation, whether well fed or hungry, whether living in plenty or in want. (Philippians 4:12)

376. I can do everything through Him who gives me strength. (Philippians 4:13)

377. And my God will meet all my needs according to His glorious riches in Christ Jesus. (Philippians 4:19)

378. I am praying that I may live a life worthy of the Lord and may please Him in every way: bearing fruit in every good work, growing in the Knowledge of God. (Colossians 1:10)

379. God has rescued me from the dominion of darkness and brought me into the Kingdom of the son he loves. (Colossians 1:13)

380. In Christ I have redemption and the forgiveness of sins. (Colossians 1:14)

381. By Him all things were created: Things in heaven and on earth, visible and invisible, whether thrones or powers or rulers or authorities, all things were created by Him and for Him. (Colossians 1:16)

382. Christ in me, the hope of glory. (Colossians 1:27)

383. I proclaim Him, admonishing and teaching everyone with all wisdom so that I may present everyone perfect in Christ. To this end I strenuously contend

with all the energy Christ so powerfully works in me. (Colossians 1:28-29)

384. I am rooted and built up in Him; strengthened in the faith as I was taught and overflowing with thankfulness. (Colossians 2:7)

385. I have been raised with Christ therefore I set my heart on things above, where Christ is seated at the right hand of God. (Colossians 3:1)

386. I will set my mind on things above, not on earthly things. (Colossians 3:2)

387. I have died, and my life is now hidden with Christ in God. (Colossians 3:3)

388. When Christ, who is my life, appears, then also I will appear with Him in glory. (Colossians 3:4)

389. I will put to death, therefore, whatever belongs to my earthly nature: sexual immorality, impurity, lust, evil desires and greed, which is idolatry. (Colossians 3:5)

390. As one of God's chosen people, holy and dearly loved, I will clothe myself with compassion, kindness, humility, gentleness and patience. (Colossians 3:12)

391. I will forgive whatever grievances I may have with others. Forgiving as the Lord forgave me. (Colossians 3:13)

392. And over all these virtues I put on love, which binds them all together in perfect unity. (Colossians 3:14)

393. I will let the peace of Christ rule in my heart, since as member of one body I've been called to peace. And to be thankful. (Colossians 3:15)

394. I will allow the word of Christ to dwell in me richly as I teach and admonish others with all wisdom, And as I sing psalms, hymns and spiritual songs. I will do it with gratitude in my heart to God. (Colossians 3:16)

395. Whatever I do, whether in word or deed, I will do it in the name of the Lord Jesus, giving thanks to God the Father through him. (Colossians 3:17)

396. Whatever I do, I will work at it with all my heart, as working for the Lord, not for men. (Colossians 3:23)

397. It is the Lord Christ that I am serving. Therefore, I know I will receive an inheritance from the Lord as a reward. (Colossians 3:24)

398. I will devote myself to prayer, being watchful and thankful. (Colossians 4:2)

399. I will be wise in the way I act toward outsiders; making the most of every opportunity. (Colossians 4:5)

400. I will let my conversation be always full of grace,

seasoned with salt, so that I may know how to answer everyone. (Colossians 4:6)

401. God did not call me to be impure, but to live a holy life. (1 Thessalonians 4:7)

402. The Lord Himself will come down from Heaven, with a loud command, with the voice of the archangel and with the trumpet call of God, and the dead in Christ will rise first. After that, we who are alive and are left will be caught up together with them in the clouds to meet the Lord in the air. And so, we will be with the Lord forever. Therefore, I will encourage others with these words. (1 Thessalonians 4:16-18)

403. I will warn those who are idle, encourage the timid, help the weak and be patient with everyone. (1 Thessalonians 5:14)

404. I will be joyful always. (1 Thessalonians 5:16)

405. I will pray continually. (1 Thessalonians 5:17)

406. I will give thanks in all circumstances for this is God's will for me in Christ. (1 Thessalonians 5:18)

407. I will pray that the message of the Lord may spread rapidly and be honored. (2 Thessalonians 3:1)

408. My Lord is faithful, and He will strengthen and protect me from the evil one. (2 Thessalonians 3:3)

409. The goal of God's command is love, which comes

from a pure heart and a good conscience and a sincere faith. (1 Timothy 1:5)

410. Now I give honor and glory to the Lord Jesus Christ forever and ever. For He is king eternal, immortal, invisible, the only God. Amen. (2 Timothy 1:17)

411. I will make requests, prayers, intercession and thanksgiving for everyone. (1 Timothy 2:1)

412. I will pray for kings and all those in authority. That I may live a peaceful and quiet life in all godliness and holiness. This is good and pleases God my Savior. (1 Timothy 2:2-3)

413. There is but one God and one mediator between God and men, the man Christ Jesus. (1 Timothy 2:5)

414. I will lift up holy hands in prayer, without anger or disputing. (1 Timothy 2:8)

415. I will have nothing to do with godless myths and old wives' tales; rather, I will train myself to be Godly. (1 Timothy 4:7)

416. My physical training is of some value, but my godliness has value for all things, holding promise for both the present life and the life to come. (1 Timothy 4:8)

417. I will set an example for the believers in speech, in life, in love, in faith and in purity. (1 Timothy 4:12)

418. I will devote myself to the public reading of scripture, to preaching and to teaching. (1 Timothy 4:13)

419. I will provide for my relatives, and specially for my immediate family, for if I don't, I deny the faith and are worse than an unbeliever. (1 Timothy 5:8)

420. Godliness with contentment is a great gain for me. (1 Timothy 6:6)

421. I will pursue righteousness, godliness, faith, love, endurance and gentleness. (1 Timothy 6:11)

422. I will fight the good fight of faith and take hold of the eternal life to which I was called when I made my good confession in the presence of many witnesses. (1 Timothy 6:12)

423. God did not give me a spirit of timidity, but a spirit of power, of love and of self-discipline. (2 Timothy 1:7)

424. I am not ashamed, because I know whom I have believed, and am convinced that He is able to guard what I have entrusted to Him for that day. (2 Timothy 1:12)

425. I will endure hardship like a good soldier of Christ Jesus. (2 Timothy 2:4)

426. I will do my best to present myself to God as one approved, a workman who does not need to be

ashamed and who correctly handles the word of truth. (2 Timothy 2:15)

427. All scripture is God's breathed and is useful for me for teaching, rebuking, correcting and training in righteousness, so that I may be thoroughly equipped for every good work. (2 Timothy 3:16-17)

428. In view of Christ appearing and His Kingdom, I have received this charge: To preach the word; be prepared in season and out of season; correct, rebuke and encourage with great patience and careful instruction. (2 Timothy 4:1-2)

429. In all situations, I will endure hardship, do the work of an evangelist, and discharge all the duties of my ministry. (2 Timothy 4:5)

430. I have fought the good fight, I have finished the race, I have kept the faith. (2 Timothy 4:7)

431. Now there is in store for me the crown of righteousness, which the Lord, the righteous judge, will award to me on that day. (2 Timothy 4:8)

432. In everything I will set an example by doing what is good. In my teaching I will show integrity, seriousness and soundness of speech that cannot be condemned, so that those who oppose me may be ashamed because they have nothing bad to say about me. (Titus 2:7-8)

433. My love for Christ has given me great joy and

encouragement and it has refreshed the hearts of the saints. (Philemon 1:7)

434. God has sent angels ministering spirits to me because I have inherited salvation. (Hebrews 1:14)

435. Jesus now crowned with glory and honor, because he suffered death, I now by the grace of God will not taste death because he tasted it for me. (Hebrews 2:9)

436. For every house is built by someone, but God is the builder of everything. (Hebrews 3:4)

437. For the Word of God is living and active. Sharper than any double-edged sword, it penetrates even to dividing my soul and spirit, joints and marrow; it judges the thoughts and attitudes of my heart. (Hebrews 4:12)

438. Nothing in all creation is hidden from God's sight. (Hebrews 4:13)

439. I have a high priest who is able to sympathize with my weaknesses. He has been tempted in every way, just as I have but without sin. (Hebrews 4:15)

440. I will approach the throne of grace with confidence, so that I may receive mercy and grace to help me in my time of need. (Hebrews 4:16)

441. God is able to save me completely because through

Him He is always living to intercede for me. (Hebrews 7:25)

442. God has placed His laws in my mind and has written them on my heart. He says I will be your God, and you will be my people. (Hebrews 8:10)

443. God has forgiven my wickedness and He will remember my sins no more. (Hebrews 8:12)

444. Without the shedding of His blood I have no forgiveness. (Hebrews 9:22)

445. It is destined for me to die once then to face judgment. (Hebrews 9:27)

446. With confidence I will enter the most Holy place by the blood of Jesus. (Hebrews 10:19)

447. By a new and living way Jesus opened for me through the curtain, that is His body. (Hebrews 10:20)

448. Because I have a high priest over the house of God I will draw near to God with a sincere heart in full assurance of faith, having my heart sprinkled to cleanse me from a guilty conscience and having my body washed with pure water. (Hebrews 10:21-22)

449. I will hold unswervingly to the hope I profess, that he who promised is faithful. (Hebrews 10:23)

450. I will consider how I can spur others on toward love and good deeds. (Hebrews 10:24)

451. I will not give up meeting together, as some are in the habit of doing, but I will encourage others, and all the more as I see the day approaching. (Hebrews 10:25)

452. If I deliberately keep on sinning after receiving the knowledge of truth, no sacrifice for my sins is left, but only a fearful expectation of judgment and of raging fire that will consume the enemies of God. (Hebrews 10:26-27

453. God has said "it is mine to avenge; I will repay." (Hebrews 10:30)

454. Faith is sure of what I hope for and certain of what I do not see. (Hebrews 11:1)

455. Without faith it is impossible for me to please God because when I come to him, I must believe that He exists then He will reward me if I earnestly seek Him. (Hebrews 11:6)

456. Because I am surrounded by a great cloud of witnesses, I will throw off everything that hinders and the sin that so easily entangles me, and I will run with perseverance the race God has marked out for me. (Hebrews 12:1)

457. I will fix my eyes on Jesus, the author and perfecter of my faith, who for the joy set before Him endured the cross, scorning its shame, and sat down at the right hand of the throne of God. (Hebrews 12:2)

458. Our fathers disciplined us for a little while as they thought best; but God disciplines us for our good, that we may share in His holiness. (Hebrews 12:10)

459. I will make every effort to live in peace with all men and to be holy; without holiness no one will see the Lord. (Hebrews 12:14)

460. Therefore, since I am receiving a Kingdom that cannot be shaken, I will be thankful and worship God acceptably with reverence and awe. (Hebrews 12:28)

461. "My God is a consuming fire." (Hebrews 12:29)

462. I will not forget to entertain strangers, for by doing so I may be entertaining angels without knowing it. (Hebrews 13:2)

463. I will remember those in prison as if I were a fellow prisoner, and those who are mistreated as if I myself was suffering. (Hebrews 13:3)

464. My marriage should be honored by me, and the marriage bed kept pure, for God will judge the adulterer and all the sexually immoral. (Hebrews 13:4)

465. He will never leave me or forsake me. (Hebrews 13:5)

466. I will say with confidence, "The Lord is my helper;

I will not be afraid. What can man do to me?" (Hebrews 13:6)

467. Jesus Christ is the same yesterday and today and forever. (Hebrews 13:8)

468. Through Jesus, I will continually offer to God a sacrifice of praise. The fruit of my lips will confess His name. (Hebrews 13:15)

469. I will not forget to do good and to share with others, for with such sacrifices God is pleased. (Hebrews 13:16)

470. I will obey my leaders and submit to their authority. They keep watch over me as men who must give an account. I will obey them so that their work will be a joy, not a burden, for that would be of no advantage to me. (Hebrews 13:17)

471. I will consider it pure joy, whenever I face trials of many kinds. (James 1:2)

472. The testing of my faith will develop perseverance. (James 1:3)

473. When I lack wisdom, I will ask God, who gives generously to all without finding fault. (James 1:5)

474. When I ask, I will believe and not doubt, because he who doubts is like a wave of the sea, blown and tossed by the wind. (James 1:6)

475. Blessed I am when I persevere under trial, because

when I have stood the test, I will receive a crown of life, that God has promised to those who love him. (James 1:12)

476. When I am tempted, I will not say "God is tempting me." For God cannot be tempted by evil, nor does He tempt anyone. (James 1:13)

477. Every good and perfect gift is from above, coming down from the Father of heavenly lights, who does not change like shifting shadows. (James 1:1:17)

478. I will take note to be quick to listen, slow to speak and slow to become angry, for a man's anger does not bring about the righteous life that God desires. (James 1:19-20)

479. I will not merely listen to the word, and so deceive myself. I will do what it says. (James 1:22)

480. Religion that God our Father accepts as pure and faultless is this: To look after orphans and widows in their distress and to keep oneself from being polluted by the world. (James 1:27)

481. As the body without the spirit is dead, so faith without deeds is dead. (James 2:26)

482. The wisdom that comes from heaven for me is first of all pure; then peaceful, loving, considerate, submissive, full of mercy and good fruit, impartial and sincere. (James 3:17

483. I will submit myself to God, resist the Devil, and he will flee from me. (James 4:7)

484. I will come near to God, and then He will come near to me. (James 4:8)

485. I will not swear not by heaven or by earth or by anything else. I will let my "Yes" be yes, and my "No" be no, otherwise I will be condemned. (James 5:12)

486. If I am sick, I will call on the elders to anoint me with oil in the name of the Lord. (James 5:14)

487. The prayer offered in faith will make me well. The Lord will raise me up. If I have sinned, God will forgive me. (James 5:15)

488. Therefore, I will confess my sins with others and pray with others so I may be healed. The prayer of a righteous man is powerful and effective. (James 5:16)

489. Just as He who called me is holy, so I will be holy in all I do. (1 Peter 1:15)

490. For it is written: "Be holy, because I am holy." (2 Peter 1:16)

491. Now that I have been purified by obeying the truth. I will love all my brothers deeply, from the heart. (1 Peter 1:22)

492. I have been born again, not of perishable seed, but

of imperishable, through the living and enduring word of God. (1 Peter 1:23)

493. Like a newborn baby I will crave the pure spiritual milk, so that by it I may grow up in my salvation. (1 Peter 2:2)

494. I have tasted that the Lord is good. (1 Peter 2:3)

495. I am a living stone, being built into a spiritual house to be a holy priesthood, offering spiritual sacrifices acceptable to God through Jesus Christ. (1 Peter 2:5)

496. I am part of the chosen people, a royal priesthood, a holy nation, a people belonging to God, that I may declare the praises of him who called me out of darkness into his wonderful light. (1 Peter 2:9)

497. By His wounds I have been healed. (1 Peter 2:24)

498. For I was once like a sheep going astray, but now I have returned to the Shepherd and overseer of my soul. (1 Peter 2:25)

499. For the eyes of the Lord are on the righteous and his ears are attentive to their prayer, but the face of the Lord is against those who do evil." (1 Peter 3:12)

500. I will love others deeply, because love covers a multitude of sins. (1 Peter 4:8)

501. I will offer hospitality to others without grumbling. (1 Peter 4:9)

502. When I suffer as a Christian, I will not be ashamed, but I will praise God that I bear his name. (1 Peter 4:16)

503. I will shepherd God's flock that is under my care, serving as an overseer, not because I must, but because I am willing, as God wants me to be; not greedy for money but eager to serve. (1 Peter 5:2)

504. I will not be lording it over those entrusted to me, but I will be an example to the flock. (1 Peter 5:3)

505. I will cast all my anxiety upon Him, because He cares for me. (1 Peter 5:7)

506. I will be self-controlled and alert. My enemy the Devil prowls around like a roaring lion looking for someone to devour. (1 Peter 5:8)

507. With the Lord, a day is like a thousand years, and a thousand years are like a day. (2 Peter 3:8)

508. God is not slow in keeping His promise as some understand slowness. He is patient with me, not wanting anyone to perish, but everyone to come to repentance. (2 Peter 3:9)

509. In keeping with His promise, I am looking forward to a new heaven and a new earth, the home of righteousness. (2 Peter 3:13)

510. This is the message I have heard from him and

declare to everyone: God is light; in Him there is no darkness at all. (1 John 1:5)

511. If I claim I have fellowship with Him yet walk in the darkness, I lie and do not live by the truth. (1 John 1:6)

512. But if I walk in the light, as He is in the light, I have fellowship with others, and the blood of Jesus, His son purifies me from all sin. (1 John 1:7)

513. If I claim to be without sin, I deceive myself and the truth is not in me. (1 John 1:8)

514. If I confess my sins, He is faithful and just and will forgive my sins and purify me from all unrighteousness. (1 John 1:9)

515. If I claim I have not sinned, I make Him a liar and his word have no place in my life. (l John 1:10)

516. I will not love the world or anything in the world. For if I love the world the love of the Father is not in me. (1 John 2:15)

517. For everything in the world, the cravings of sinful man, the lust of his eyes and the boasting of what he has and does, comes not from the Father but from the world. (1 John 2:16)

518. The world and its desires pass away, but I choose to be the man who does the will of God so I can live forever. (1 John 2:17)

519. I have an anointing from the holy one. (1 John 2:20)

520. The anointing that I have received from Him teaches me all things, is real, not counterfeit, it teaches me to remain in Him. (1 John 2:27)

521. I know I am a child of God! And that is what I am! The reason the world does not know me is that it did not know Him. (1 John 3:1)

522. I know that when He appears, I will be like Him, for I will see Him as He is. I have this hope therefore I purify myself, just as He is pure. (1 John 3:3)

523. No one who lives in Him keeps on sinning. No one who continues to sin has either seen Him or known Him. (1 John 3:6)

524. If I do what is sinful, I am of the Devil, because the Devil has been sinning from the beginning. The reason the son of God appeared was to destroy the Devil's work. (1 John 3:8)

525. This is how I know what love is: Jesus Christ laid down his life for me. I ought to lay down my life for my brothers. (1 John 3:16)

526. And this is His command: to believe in the name of His son, Jesus Christ, and to love others as He commanded us. (1 John 3:22)

527. The one who is in me is greater than the one who is in the world. (1 John 4:4)

528. If 1 don't love I do not know God, because God is love. (1 John 4:8)

529. There is no fear in love. But perfect love drives out my fear. (1 John 4:18)

530. And this is the testimony: God has given me eternal life, and this life is in His son. (1 John 5:11)

531. I have the son therefore I have life; for he who does not have the son of God does not have life. (1 John 5:12)

532. This is the confidence I have in approaching God: That if I ask anything according to His will, He hears me. (1 John 5:14)

533. And if I know that He hears me, whatever I ask I know that I have what I asked of him. (1 John 5:15)

534. And this is love that I walk in obedience to His commands. As I have heard from the beginning, His command is that I walk in love. (2 John 1:6)

535. If I run ahead and do not continue in the teaching of Christ, I do not have God; whoever continues in the teaching has both the Father and the Son. (2 John 1:9)

536. I am praying that I may enjoy good health and that all may go well with me, even as my soul is getting along well. (3 John 1:2)

537. I have no greater joy than to hear that my children are walking in the truth. (3 John 1:4)

538. I must contend for the faith it has been entrusted to me and all the saints. (Jude 1:3)

539. I will build myself up in the most holy faith and pray in the spirit. (Jude 1:20)

540. God has made me to be a Kingdom and a priest to serve him. To Him be glory and power forever and ever! Amen. (Revelation 1:6)

541. "He is the alpha and the omega," says the Lord, "who is, and who was, and who is to come, the almighty." (Revelation 1:8)

542. I will not be afraid. He said I am the first and the last. I am the living one. I was dead, and behold I am alive for ever and ever! And I hold the keys of death and Hades. (Revelation 1:18)

543. I will be faithful, even to the point of death, and then He will give me a crown of life. (Revelation 2:10)

544. I will overcome and do God's will to the end. He then will give me authority over the nations. (Revelation 2:26)

545. If I overcome, I will be dressed in white. He will never blot out my name from the book of life but will acknowledge my name before my Father and his angels. (Revelation 3:5)

546. God has opened a door for me that no one can shut. (Revelation 3:8)

547. Anyone who is lukewarm – neither hot or cold – I will spit you out of my mouth says the Lord. (Revelation 3:16)

548. God is standing at the door and knocking, when I hear His voice, I will open the door and let him in. He then will eat with me and be with me. (Revelation 3:20)

549. Then I heard a loud voice in heaven say: "Now have come the salvation and the power and the Kingdom of our God, and the authority of His Christ. For the accuser of our brothers, who accuse them before our God day and night has been hurled down. (Revelation 12:10)

550. I will overcome the Devil by my testimony. (Revelation 12:11)

551. I will rejoice and be glad and give Him glory! For the wedding of the lamb has come, and His bride has made herself ready. (Revelation 19:7)

552. The Book of Life was opened. The dead were judged according to what they had done as recorded in the books. (Revelation 20:12)

553. If anyone's name was not found written in the Book of Life, he was thrown into the lake of fire. (Revelation 20:15)

554. God will wipe every tear from my eyes. There will be no more death or mourning or crying or pain, for the old order of things will pass away. (Revelation 21:4)

555. He who is seated on the throne said, "I am making everything new." (Revelation 21:5)

556. If I remain thirsty, He will give me to drink without cost from the spring of the water of life. (Revelation 21:6)

557. If I overcome, I will inherit all of this, and I will be his son and He will be my God. (Revelation 21:7)

558. But the cowardly, the unbelieving, the vile, the murderers, the sexually immoral, those who practice magic arts, the idolaters and all liars – their place will be in the fiery lake of burning sulfur. (Revelation 21:8)

559. Jesus is coming soon! His reward is with Him, and He will give to everyone according to what he has done. (Revelation 22:12)

PRAYERS

BREAKING OF CURSES

- Today, Jesus, I declare that you are my Lord and Savior. I believe that you died on the cross for my sins. I thank you that you took my sins and curses to the cross and that you became a curse for me.

- Today I renounce in Jesus' name any cursed placed on my life. I ask that the blood of Jesus cleanse me and set me free in these areas.

- I repent, renounce, and take ownership of any curse, gossip, negative words, anger, and judgment that I have spoken against people knowingly or unknowingly. Dear Lord, I am so sorry for sinning. Please forgive me.

- I release myself from these words, the power of these words, and the power and effect that they had on me and others in Jesus' name.

- I bless those who curse me.

BREAKING GENERATIONAL CURSES

Dear Lord Jesus, I come before you today and acknowledge that you are my Lord Savior. I believe you died on the cross for my sins and the sins of my ancestors. You took sin and curses to the cross. On the cross, you exchanged curses for blessings, and defeated Satan and his powers.

- I confess, repent renounce, and take ownership of sins and curses in our family line (mother and father).

- I confess, repent and take ownership of all ungodly thoughts, negativity, gossip, bitter words, vows, judgments, curses, ungodly covenants and ungodly beliefs in my life and from my ancestors. (i.e. pride, anger, violence, fear, shame, bitterness, witchcraft, and hatred of men and women).

- I confess, repent and take ownership of all rejection in me and from ancestors.

- I confess, repent and take ownership of all addictions in me and my ancestors (i.e. alcohol, nicotine, drugs, food, pornography, TV, video games, computer, and other false comforts).

- I confess, repent and take ownership of known and unknown sexual sin in me and ancestors (i.e. adultery, fornications, homosexuality/lesbianism, incest, masturbation, prostitution, rape, sexual abuse, bestiality, obsessions, and perversions).

- I confess, repent and take ownership of the destruction of marriage and family through divorce.

- I confess, repent and take ownership of the curse of Freemasonry in my family line, by me or from my ancestors – every word, action, agreement from the 1st degree to the 33rd degree of Freemasonry.

- I repent, renounce and take ownership of any connection by me or my ancestors of being part of an ungodly organization, college fraternity, or sorority. I renounce all vows, secret handgrips, traditions, emblems, and badges associated with those organizations and the effects that these curses have had on my family and me.

- I confess, repent, and take ownership of untimely physical death and spiritual death (i.e. abortion, death in the womb, premature death, sudden and traumatic death, suicide, murder, war, unresolved grief, anger, bitterness, resentment, fear, loss of dreams and hope).

- I confess, repent and take ownership of the effects of guilt, false guilt, fear and feelings on myself and from my ancestors.

- I confess, repent and take ownership of the effects of war on me and from my ancestors (i.e. loss of family, home, laud, possessions, finances, health, destruction and pride).

- I confess, repent and take ownership of all religious restrictions and constrictions from a Christian church or denomination, or from a different religion, by myself or from ancestors (i.e. legalism, false doctrine, spiritual abuse, oaths, vows, rituals).

- I confess, repent, and take ownership of all involvement with the occult by me and my ancestors. I recognize that supernatural knowledge and power not coming from God is evil. I renounce every agreement, covenant, and blood covenant involved with the occult that has affected me.

- I confess, repent and take ownership where my family's line has not taught the ways of God to me and my ancestors (i.e. loss of Godly blessings, heritage, and inheritance, and reaping the consequences of sin, sickness, poverty).

- I confess, repent, and take ownership of any ungodly soul ties in my life and my ancestor's life.

- I confess, repent, and take ownership of ungodly

attitudes, practices, and involvement by me and from my ancestor's cultural background (i.e. prejudice, superiority, pride ungodly things in cultures, and shame).

- I confess, repent and take ownership of all hereditary illnesses, disease, and weaknesses.

- I confess, repent and take ownership in generational financial areas, and in my finances, that I resolve to be obedient to the Lord in the areas of finance, tithes and offerings.

- Please forgive me Lord for blaming you.

- Please forgive me Lord for blaming others.

- Please forgive me Lord for blaming myself.

- I release myself, my family and my ancestors from curses and generational curses in the name of Jesus Christ.

- In the name of Jesus Christ, we bind any demonic spirits and powers involved in curses and generational curses in my life, and I command Satan to loose his hold over my life, my family and all areas of life.

- I receive your forgiveness and freedom today, Lord, in Jesus' name.

- Lord, I ask that you release the favor and blessings

in my life that were prevented by these curses operating.

- Lord, I promise to follow you every day of my life. I promise to be your servant and part of your flock. I will delight myself always in you. Amen!

THE PRESIDENT

- Dear Father, in Jesus' name I lift up our president to you. I know that our leader's heart is in your hand, so I ask you to guide the head of our nation in the way you would have him to go.

- Father, I pray that you would surround our president with wise councilmen and women of integrity who place your agenda and the good of this nation above their own and whose motives are for that which is right.

- I pray that you would give our leader discernment, understanding and knowledge so that our nation may know stability internally and abroad.

- I give thanks for our president according to your word and thank you for working in and through his leadership so that we might lead peaceful lives in godliness and honesty.

THE CONGRESS

- Dear Father, I come to you in the mighty name of Jesus, thanking you and praising you for our great nation. I thank you for the plan you gave to our forefathers by which to govern our nation and for the division of powers so that our destiny does not rest in the hands of one person.

- In praying for those in authority, I therefore lift up our Congress (both the House of Representatives and the Senate). I pray that, by your power, our legislative body would make laws that are just.

- Father, I ask you to give them wisdom to make decisions that would strengthen and prosper our nation. I desire that they would make right decisions concerning the politics, the social welfare and the economics of our nation.

- I pray that you would cause congress to be motivated more by your hand than by partisan or personal concerns.

DECISIONS IN NATIONAL CRISIS

- Father God, in the name of Jesus, I pray that you would direct the leaders of this nation in times of crisis. Grant them wisdom and understanding and help them to respond quickly and effectively to each situation. May divinely directed decisions be on their lips, and may they do that which is right in your sight. May they follow your will to direct our nation in the paths of peace and safety.

- Unite all response agencies in an organized and

harmonious fashion to bring quick and effective resolve to the demands of this crisis.

- Empower us as United States citizens to do our part, financially, physically, emotionally and spiritually to support all who have been affected by this tragedy.

- I pray that you encourage and strengthen our nation. Surround us with your love and mercy. Bring peace and comfort to all those who are suffering as a result of this crisis.

THE ECONOMY

- Dear Father, in the name of the Lord Jesus, I pray for our nation's economy I know that even more than a strong military, a strong economy helps keep a nation powerful.

- Father, I pray that you would raise up people of skill and wisdom who will affect the economy of our nation. Give them inspired ideas and a voice with the powers that be.

- Cause congress to vote aright in these matters. Give them foresight so that provision might be made for our nation's future, not just its present.

- Father, as the people of our nation continue to finance the preaching of the gospel and help the poor all over the world, I pray that you would continue to prosper us more and more. .

SUPREME COURT JUSTICES

- Father, in the name of Jesus, I bring our Supreme Court justices before you. Knowing that they are appointed of man, I pray that you would influence the selection of each new replacement. May they be people who will judge rightly in every matter brought before them.

- As our supreme court makes its decisions, I pray that its decrees would be your decrees. I desire that, by your hand, godly justice would rise up within our justices and that they would make rulings in line with your will.

- I pray that they would set a standard of justice and balance for the judicial office at large, not only on a national level but for every adjudicator in our nation.

- We give you thanks, dear Father, knowing it is your good pleasure and will to work in every level of government.

ELECTION OF GODLY LEADERS

- Father, I desire to vote intelligently in all elections. I pray that you will bring to light the things I need to know so that I may vote in line with your plan, will and purpose.

- May things not only come to light for the Christian community, but may things be made clear to the unbelieving community as well. I pray that people will vote using wisdom and demanding honesty and uprightness from their politicians.

- Dear Father, in the name of Jesus, may the citizens of our nation become so weary of sin and degradation in our nation's leaders that they will begin to seek out godly leaders to represent them in every level of government. Give such leaders favor with the public and the media.

- Father make our nation a fragrance in the earth, a force to be reckoned with, a hand extended to those in need.

NATIONAL MORALITY

- Father, I know that the spirit of the world creeps into the body of Christ almost unawares sometimes, and before we know it, we can so easily be led astray and caught up in worldly actions (at times so subtly we don't even recognize what has happened to us).

- So, in the name of Jesus, I pray that you would raise up a voice in our nation that would rally the body of Christ and cause us to become the standard bearers to such a degree that we would profoundly affect the morality of our nation.

SCHOOLS

- Father, in the name of Jesus, I pray that you would

ignite our schools with holy fire, that you would continue to embolden our Christian youth to take a stand with their peers and show them the way, Jesus Christ. May they boldly speak the word so that you may stretch forth your hand to heal and do signs and wonders in the name of Jesus Christ.

- May there be such a move of your grace and power in our nation's school systems that alcohol, drugs, guns, pornography and illicit sexual activity cease to be issues. May the fear of the Lord prevail in our schools to the degree that no one would dare to transgress.

THE EDUCATIONAL SYSTEM

- Dear Father, in the name of Jesus, I pray for all those who are in authority in our national educational system. I pray that the decisions they make would be by your guidance.

- Please help those in authority see that "separation of church and state" does not mean godless education.

- May there be such a revival in our nation that those in power must acknowledge that which is right in your sight.

- May our goal be not only to understand the students, but to bring them to understanding both on a moral and intellectual level.

- Cause our educational system to be preeminent in the world. And may discipline and respect be restored to our nation's school.

NATIONAL PATRIOTISM

- Father, I pray in Jesus' name that you would restore a social conscience to our nation.

- I pray that we would again see the value of teaching our children the virtue of being good citizens--to not only live for the good of the individual but the good of others as well.

- Dear Father, I desire to see our nation restored to godly integrity and excellence, so that our children and our citizens can be proud of their nation and proud to be called citizens of it.

- In recognizing our duty to God and our country, keep us mindful to pray for our nation not only in our churches and our homes, but also in the quietness of our daily lives.

NATIONAL PROTECTION

- Most high God, I come to you in the name of Jesus, asking for divine protection for the people of this nation. I pray for the safety of every man, women and child. Keep us from harm's way and provide protection from plans of destruction that our enemies have plotted. Stop strategies of destruction that our enemies would try to evoke.

- Give wisdom, understanding and discernment to those who provide protection. Help us to be watchful and alert to signs of wrongdoing.

- Provide insight to national and local authorities on ways to guard, defend and insure the safety of all American citizens both at home and abroad. Help us to unite with government leaders and law enforcement personnel in making this country a safe place to live, work and play; allowing Americans to enjoy freedom without fear.

PEACE

- Dear Father, I clearly see that it is your will for us to dwell in peace and safety. In obedience to your word I continue to pray, in the name of the Lord Jesus, that those in authority will make decisions to keep our nation safe, just as I pray for peace in other nations.

- I pray our nation would be a blessing to Israel that we might continue to be blessed.

- I pray that the righteousness of our nation would continue to finance the preaching of the Gospel in the entire world. I pray that our sending and our giving would increase.

- May our nation continue to help nations that are in trouble and are less fortunate than we are.

- I ask you to make our nation a blessing to all the nations of the earth.

THE MILITARY

- Thank you, Lord, for the men and women of our armed forces. Protect them as they protect us. Defend them as they defend us. Encourage and strengthen their spirit, soul and body in the execution of their duties and responsibilities. May they be mentally and physically strong when required to face the challenges of combat. Under gird them with your spirit and might when they are called upon to endure the hardships of battle.

- I pray that nothing would take them by surprise but that they would be aware of all potential aggression. Enable them to curtail hostile actions before they start.

- Reveal to military leaders the strategies and plots that enemies would wage. Give leaders wisdom and insight in all decisions. May response to any aggression by enemies of this nation be swift, accurate and effective.

- Father give our military favor with the governmental agencies of this country. I pray that our Congress would appropriate sufficient funds to keep our nation's military preeminent in the world.

- Thank you, Lord, for providing America with the best led, trained and equipped military force in the world today. Fill them with your saving grace and the gospel of peace that they may be shining witnesses of Your love, in the name of Jesus.

THE FAMILIES OF OUR MILITARY

- Father, in the name of the Lord Jesus, I also lift up to you in prayer the families of our military. I pray that the gospel will extend to them, that they might know him and the power of his resurrection.

- Father, I desire that these families might be a prayer force for our nation and our military.

- May they know abundance and not lack. May they be well provided for and well taken care of. Father give them the courage of warriors. May the peace that passes understanding sustain them in seasons of separation.

- Comfort them with your word that they might have faith to see their sons, daughters, husbands and wives returned to them in wholeness and safety.

PROTECTION FROM TERRORISM

- Father, in the name of the Lord Jesus, I pray that you prevent the destructive forces of terrorism directed against our nation. Provide protection from evil attacks and stop the aggressors that attempt to bring destruction to our nation and people. May your hand of protection keep us safe.

- I stand against the spirit of fear that accompanies the cowardice acts of terrorism. Allow our fear to turn to trust in you. May knowledge of terrorist planned attacks be revealed to those who provide our national and international security. Help those in power to act swiftly to avert all danger, protecting American lives and property.

- Provide strength, courage and wisdom to the protectors of this nation to administer their duties. Give wisdom and insight to our government and everyone involved in the elimination of terrorism. Provide instruction in the development of effective and efficient anti-terrorist strategies that will give us an advantage against our aggressors allowing the country to remain safe and secure.

- I pray that the instigators of terrorism recognize the evil of their ways, and repent and denounce their cowardice acts of destruction against humanity. Without repentance, may they reap the consequences of their actions and may the fear of our retaliation be greater than their hatred of democracy.

- Guide us in efforts to seek out and eradicate

these merchants of death. Reveal the names of those responsible and in allegiance with terrorist organizations to our authorities. Enable the military to become swift, powerful and accurate in any action of retaliation.

- Lord, help us to understand lifestyle changes that might be necessary to ensure our protection. Grant patience and tolerance to us in adapting to the safety precautions and measures that we might experience. Enable us to realize that the cost of inconvenience is a small price to pay for the safety of our families and of our nation.

NATIONAL DISASTER

- Father, in the name of the Lord Jesus, please direct our rescue workers in their labors that survivors of disasters will be found in time. Help those in authority to make the right decisions. Show them ways to avoid and avert such tragedy in the future.

- I pray that in the face of this tragedy, the gospel will be preached.

- I pray grieving families would be comforted.

IN TIME OF WAR

- Father, I come to you, in the name of our Lord Jesus, to lift up in prayer this present military action. Father, I pray that there might be a quick resolution to this action and that truth and righteousness would prevail.

- May you guide, bless and protect all those engaged in this conflict. Heal the physical and spiritual wounds that may be inflicted.

- Father, the gospel of the kingdom must be preached to this nation. I pray that what Satan has intended and devised to hinder the gospel you will turn to our good, that the gospel will go into this nation unimpeded.

- Let all who hear Your Word turn to you for guidance, courage and hope.

TYPES OF PRAYERS IN THE NEW TESTAMENT

- Prayer of confession of sin 1 JOHN 1:9

- Prayer of confessing our faults JAMES 5:16

- Prayer of agreement MATTHEW 18:19

- Prayer of faith JAMES 5:15

- Prayer of binding MATTHEW 16:19

- Prayer of loosing MATTHEW 16:19

- Praying in the Spirit EPHESIANS 6:18

- Praying in the Spirit with understanding. 1 CORINTHIANS 14:15

- Prayer of thanksgiving PHILIPPIANS 4:6

- Prayer of intercession 1 TIMOTHY 2:1

- Prayer of general supplication PHILIPPIANS 4:6

GETTING ANSWERS

SEVEN SPIRITUAL LAWS FOR ANSWERED PRAYERS

Believing is the first step and confession seals the believing. Believing and confessing are spiritual laws that create a supernatural result for the believer and the confessor. Just as there are natural laws of gravity, aerodynamics and life and death, there are also laws of the spirit (Romans 8:2), including spiritual guidelines for prayer.

Praying means to ask or to form words from your heart and speak them as a petition and request before God

LAW 1—YOU MUST ASK

Christ taught that you must ask: "Ask and it will be given to you" (Luke 11:9). We use the word; ask everyday: for example: "May I ask you a question?" "Did you ask for directions?" "May I ask you a favor?" Asking involves saying something; you cannot ask with your mouth closed. While there are different forms of prayer, all prayer involves asking or petitioning God. There is a spiritual principle throughout the bible that God does nothing to meet a need for a believer on the earth until he is first asked.

- God spared Lot because Abraham petitioned God on Lot's behalf (Genesis 18)

- God spared Israel from complete destruction because Moses interceded (Exodos 32)

- King Hezekiah was given a death sentence. However when he asked God to extend his days, God added fifteen more years (Isaiah 38:5)

- When Peter was in prison with plans for his execution to take place following the Passover, the church did not cease from praying and God released an angel of the Lord to free Peter (Acts 12)

LAW 2—YOU MUST ASK IN FAITH

Each person who believes in Christ has a measure. Romans 12:3"God has dealt to each one a measure of faith." Faith is one of the nine fruits of the spirit (Galatians 5:22).

When you pray you must ask, but you must ask in faith. When exercising faith, you maintain a sense of expectation. After praying, your faith begins to tell you God has heard your prayers and he is working in your situation. Expectation helps maintain confidence in God's willingness and ability to move on your behalf.

LAW 3—YOU MUST ASK IN FAITH... NOTHING WAVERING

> *James1:6-8 "But let him ask in faith with no doubting. For he who doubts is like a wave of the sea driven and tossed by the wind. For let no man suppose that he will receive anything from the Lord; he is double-minded man, unstable in all his ways."*

Wavering would be if you said in the morning, "I believe God will do it," and before the sun was setting, you are saying, "It just looks like nothing is going to happen!" It basically means "without blending or mixing." It is the asking in faith with no withdrawal from your belief with no stagger or doubt.

LAW 4—YOU MUST BE IN FULL AGREEMENT WITH ONE ANOTHER

> *Matthew 18:19-20"Again I say that if two of you agree on earth concerning anything that they ask it will be done for them by my Father in heaven. For, where two or three are gathered together in my name, I am there in the midst of them."*

The word "agree" means together in one accord. In a group of people after someone is praying is to agree in their inner spirits with the one who is praying. Say "amen" or "so be it" or "let it be", so as to not speak varied words in all different directions. A prayer of agreement only requires two people. In the Torah, God required two or three witnesses to establish a crime (Duet. 17:6) by the agreement of two or three witnesses, every word is established or settled (Deut. 19:15). Prayer agreement must be more than agreeing with the mind or with words; it must be an agreement deep within your spirit. An assurance and unity that cannot be broken by outward circumstances that may appear to be working contrary to your prayers.

LAW 5—YOU MUST ASK THE FATHER IN JESUS NAME

Under the first covenant, Hebrew men approached God in prayer by addressing Him as the "God of Abraham, Isaac and Jacob" (Exod. 3:16; 6:3; 32:13; 33:1). These three names are the patriarchs of Faith with whom God confirmed and reconfirmed His covenant. When praying in the name of these three men, it reminds God of his everlasting promise toward the seed of Abraham.

Under the new covenant, we approach God through the name of Jesus Christ because Christ initiated a new covenant through His death and resurrection!

John 14:13-14 "Whatever you ask in my name

that I will do, that the Father will be glorified in the Son. If you ask anything in my name, I will do it."

John 15:16"You did not choose Me, but I chose you and appointed you that you should go and bear fruit, and that your fruit should remain, that whatever you ask the father in My name he may give you."

John 16:23-24"And in that day, you will ask Me nothing. Most assuredly, I say to you, whatever you ask the Father in My name He will give you. Until now you have asked nothing in My name. Ask, and you will receive, that your joy may be full. "

Always ask in His name! Christ is the heavenly high priest, ever living to make intercession for us (Hebrews 7:22-25). He is today at the right hand of God.

LAW 6—YOU MUST HOLD FAST TO YOUR CONFESSION

Hebrews 10:23"Let us hold fast the confession of our hope without wavering, for he who promised is faithful." The words "hold fast" paint the imagery of a person searching a long time for something or someone, then when suddenly finding it, they seize it without letting go. It means to hold on to your confession of Christ tightly.

Prayer consists of words, but the words are also a dynamic spiritual force. Jesus said, "The words that I speak to you are spirit and they are life" (John 6:63). How can words be "spirit"? A spirit being is invisible to the natural eye and words can be heard but are not seen (invisible) to the natural eye. A spirit can travel at the speed of thought and your words travel from earth to heaven at the speed of thought. Your words actually travel at tremendous speed and distances. So, hold fast to the words out of your mouth when you pray.

MAINTAINING YOUR CONFESSION

Picture yourself on earth praying a prayer of faith to receive a needed answer from the Lord. You have petitioned the Father in heaven and you are thanking Him for hearing your prayer. For the next several weeks, you begin to speak faith words indicating your expectation of a possible, sudden visitation from God; bringing a much-needed answer to prayer. However, the weeks turn to months and the months turn into a year. After a year passes by, your faith begins wavering and your confession changes. You begin to say, "God is not hearing me. I am weary of waiting and tired of believing...I am going to give up..." In your earthly time dimension, twelve months have passed. Scripture indicates that one day with the Lord is a thousand years, and a thousand years is as one day (Ps. 90:4; 2 Pet. 3:8). One thousand solar years consist of about 365, 250 days. These days translated into hours are 8,766,000 hours. That's a lot of time. Yet to God, this time can be equal to one day in the eternal dimension. That is why theoretically if you pray a strong prayer, and do not waver and hold on to your confession, your steadfast in your verbal agreement will come to pass.

LAW 7—YOU MUST AGREE IN LINE WITH THE WILL OF GOD

There are three types of wills on earth. There is the will of God, the will of Satan, and the will of man.

- The will of God is revealed in the word of God. The ultimate will of God is that none perish but that all come to God through repentance (2 Peter 3:9).

- The will of Satan is "to steal and to kill and to destroy" (John 10:10) and to prevent a person from turning to God through repentance.

- The will of man includes the mental and spiritual ability to choose between eternal life and eternal punishment, to follow or reject the truth and to choose between good and evil. God never forces His will upon an individual. But he provides each person the option of accepting Him by submitting his or her will to God by believing or rejecting Him by choosing to not believe.

John 3:36 says it this way: "He who believes in

the Son has everlasting life; and he who does not believe the Son shall not see life, but the wrath of God abides on him."

Satan does not play by the same rules and will use temptation, trials and other circumstances as mental and spiritual pressures to cause a person to make wrong choices.

These seven spiritual laws and principles of prayer are not complicated; they are simple enough for a child to understand. But we must always remember that we must believe and not doubt and activate all seven principles for our progress in the Lord.

Psalm 122:6 Pray for the peace of Jerusalem: "May those who love you be secure."

PRAYER

12 SIGNIFICANT PRAYER INITIATIVES

Oh, Lord God of Israel, we put our trust in you for the security of the nation of Israel. Your word declares Mount Zion will not be moved! Israel shall abide forever according to your Word. Adorn its land with Jerusalem as its undivided capital. Send your shalom down on Israel, on its land and on its people, like a wedding canopy. Surround Jerusalem and your people with your mighty warrior angels.

Give supernatural protection within and without Israel's borders. Break the scepter of every wicked ruler who plots evil against the land allotted to the righteous. Cleanse Israel's borders of violence and bloodshed, that those you love may not be tempted to do iniquity. Destroy the power and plan of every regime that threatens the peace and security of your inheritance and the possession you have given forever.

Lord as you showed favor to Esther in the evil day, we beseech you, stretch out the scepter of righteousness and justice to bring good to the upright in the land! Lead away all those who have dire plans, plots of terrorism or schemes of destruction against your people. Break apart any league among Israel's enemies who would force Israel to compromise its inheritance for the sake of peace.

Rulers of the nations have mercy on America and remember its alms and past acts of kindness for Israel and Jewish people. As you have determined to Bless those who Bless Abraham's seed, be kind to America. Take our nation by hand and cause us to walk uprightly toward your people in our generation. Prevent our leaders or people from putting a hand against your holy people or coming against Israel. Break the influence of Israel's enemies among our leaders and in our economy.

We cry out for America's destiny in your good purposes to be utterly fulfilled. We bind America as a friend to Israel and the Jewish people. We pray that America would not be named among those who would heave away Jerusalem for the sake of peace with its enemies. Turn the hearts of all our leaders as water that flows to build up Israel according to your plan. Raise up your tabernacle, which has fallen down. Set your sanctuary in their midst forever. Let all nations see that you have set Israel apart for yourself. Helper of Israel do not allow Israel's foot to be moved. Be Israel's keeper and shade at the nation's right hand. Keeping watch over it both day and night! Preserve its going out and coming in both now and forever. In the name of Jesus Christ, we pray. Amen!

12 SIGNIFICANT PRAYER INITIATIVES

1. **Bow your knees in Prayer** (Ephesians 3:14) "For this reason I bow my knees to the Father of our Lord Jesus Christ"

2. **Include the Lord's Prayer** (Matthew 6:9-13)

3. **Take Quality time** (Matthew 26:40) "Could you men not keep watch with me for one hour?"

4. **Pray as long as the burden stays.** We must remove all forms of distractions and pray in deep intercession, the Holy Spirit will begin to place in your spirit certain leadings or directions toward another person or situation, thereby revealing to you who and what you have been burdened for. Never quit praying as long as your spirit remains restless. Only when the burden lifts should you arise from your prayer position.

5. **Pray Without Ceasing** (1 Thessalonians 5:16) "Pray continually." This means pray not just occasionally but constantly reoccurring.

6. **Don't Be Influenced by Surroundings.** Remember: Daniel prayed in a smelly Lion's Den (Daniel 6). Ezekiel saw the visions of God while in

exile in Babylon (Ezekiel 1:10) John, the author of the book of Revelation was banished to the desolate island of Patmos (Revelation 1:9)

7. **Pray for your Family's Protection Daily.** All family members should be included.

8. **Discern the Spiritual Sudden lies.** These came in nudges of the spirit. These inner urges have a mouth to speak to God, but not many have the ear to hear from God. Remember that the adversary comes to "steal and kill and destroy" (John 10:10)

9. **Pray in the Spirit.** The purpose of the prayer language is to change a person's inner spirit to speak to God (1 Corinthians 14:2). Being baptized in the Holy Spirit (Acts 1:5) allows the believer to pray in tongues.

10. **Conclude in Praise.** In the book of Psalms, twelve of the psalms conclude with the words, "Praise the Lord." (Psalms 104:35, 150:6, for example)

11. **Remember God Answers Prayers for His Glory.** Always emphasize "For the glory of the Son of God." "They marveled and Glorified God" (Matthew 9:8) "They glorified the God of Israel" (Matt. 15:31)

12. **Pray in the Spirit...**With the interpretation. The Holy Spirit is always eager to give you instruction. Praying in the Spirit you may go into the languages imparted to you at the time. Ask the Lord for the

interpretation you will be surprised! God desires that your words come from the wellspring of your inner being.

BECOMING WHOLE

HOW TO RECEIVE INNER HEALING

Unforgiveness will hinder or block the healing power of the Holy Spirit. It will bind you up and separate you from God's forgiving and healing power. It is vital to release those feelings that you have against others, so that the Holy Spirit's healing and forgiving power can heal and restore your soul.

Unforgiveness is a deadly poison that separates us from God's forgiveness in our own lives and gives us over to tormenting spirits. It is hard to receive healing when one is in such a position. Consider these passages in scripture concerning the deadliness of unforgiveness and bitterness in our lives:

Mark 11: 25-26 And when you stand praying,

if you hold anything against anyone, forgive him, so that your Father in Heaven may forgive you your sins.

As we can see, unforgiveness will block God's forgiveness from operating in our own lives. Inner healing requires God's forgiveness.

Matthew 18:32-35 Then the master called the servant in. You wicked servant; he said, I canceled all that debt of yours because you begged me to. Shouldn't you have had mercy on your fellow servant just as I had on you? In anger his master turned him over to the jailers to be tortured, until he should pay back all he owed. This is how my heavenly Father will treat each of you unless you forgive your brother from your heart.

Unforgiveness will put us into the hands of tormenting spirits. This is the last thing we need when we're seeking healing for our souls! As if that isn't enough, unforgiveness also puts a person in spiritual darkness and separation from God, and defiles us spiritually:

1 John 2:11 But whoever hates his brother is still in darkness and walks around in the darkness, he does not know where he is going, because the darkness has blinded him.

It is absolutely essential to release feelings of bitterness and unforgiveness in order to fully receive healing for our souls. Forgiving others will welcome the healing power of the Holy Spirit into our lives.

REALIZE WHO YOU ARE IN CHRIST

Realizing your identity in Christ is absolutely vital to our healing process. You need to know that you are a new creation in Christ, freed from the darkness of your past, forgiven of your sins, and freedom and healing are yours because of the BLOOD THAT CHRIST SHED FOR YOU! Stop feeding on lies of insecurity, guilt, and pain. (Jesus took your pain)

It is absolutely vital that we not listen or pay attention to the voice of the Devil in our minds. God's word tells us that we need to be taking every thought captive to the obedience of Christ.

> *2 Corinthians 10:4 The weapons we fight with are not the weapons of the world. On the contrary, they have divine power to demolish strongholds.*

FORGIVE YOURSELF - SEE YOURSELF AS GOD'S SEES YOU

Forgiving yourself is a vital step that we must take while seeking inner healing. We need to love and appreciate the person that Christ has made in us! It is vital to see ourselves for who we really are in Christ. If you continue to beat yourself up for past failures, after the Blood of Christ has washed them away, then you are, in reality, denying the very work of the cross! Here are a few of many good verses to meditate on in God's word!

> *Psalms 103:12 As far as the east is from the west, so far has he removed our transgressions from us.*

> *Romans 5:1 Therefore, since we have been justified through faith, we have peace with God through our Lord Jesus Christ.*

> *Isaiah 43:25 I, even I, am he who blots out your transgressions, for my own sake, and remembers your sins no more.*

> *Hebrews 10:22 Let us draw near to God with sincere heart in full assurance of faith, having our hearts sprinkled to cleanse us from a guilty conscience and having our bodies washed with pure water.*

Speak to the pain and release it into Jesus hands. Lastly, go to the pain, the emotional wound that is hidden within you, and confront it with the healing love of Christ. Knowing that Jesus has paid for your emotional wounds, hurts, pains, and sorrows, tell the inner hurt, painful memories, and emotional affliction to leave in the name of Jesus. Then call upon Jesus to remove those things from you. You might pray something like this:

"Lord Jesus, I love you, thank you for bearing my burden on the cross. I ask that you take these inner hurts, painful memories, and emotional wounds from me right now. I submit them to you and accept your peace in place of those things which I am giving up."

WORD REVELATIONS FROM THE LORD

My Beloved, I am your I am, I have come in this season to give you rest. This will be a time of rest and reflection. I am giving you a new dream; my banner of love is now upon you. Come unto me for my yoke is easy and my burden is light. I shall now give unto you a new revelation. New manna from Heaven, this will be a time of new divine connections and brand-new relationships. You will prepare my bride for my coming. Make my people strong and courageous. They must learn to take their territories with spiritual violence. I will be with them during this time. I will lead them and be their rear guard. My people all over the world will now know I am their God and shield and their defender. I will lift their heads with my glory. I am preparing their hands for battle with their enemies. I am at this time raising a remnant of new leaders that will lead a triumphal visitation of my spirit. My glory shall be in their heads. I am giving you rest for the battles ahead. You will be victorious.

My blood covers a multitude of sins. In this season I am covering my saints with my Blood so they can expand my kingdom. I am bringing power of liberty upon my people to do my work. They will do extra-ordinary things and bring many to me. This will be a time where hungry people will be satisfied by my food, celestial food. I am bridging the gap between my Jews and Gentiles and I am opening the nations to hear my good news. The Spirit of John the Baptist will indeed prepare the way for my visitation. There will be much debris, but I am detaching the old wineskin and bringing in the new wineskin. This will now be the season to put on the new garment of praise, new songs, new sound, new roar, new weapons for the war ahead, A season of breakthroughs, a season of increase, a season of fruitfulness. See I am pouring out my Spirit on those who love me and trust in me. They will be victorious in the Battles ahead. This is the time where the roar of the lion of Judah will be greater than the roar of the roaring lion of the enemy. My people will win.

The eyes of the Lord are upon the righteous. My ears are attentive unto all their cries. I am the same today as I was yesterday. I am bringing my remnant higher, but to go higher they must go deeper with me. I will then take my people there and they too will be blessed. Can you hear me calling? I am measuring my line unto the deep...Who is willing to go for me into the deep waters? Do you hear my voice? Son I am with you always through your difficult moments. Through your quiet times, every moment of your life I am with you. Your life I am with you. Your life is inscribed in the palms of my hand. Praise me in the morning; praise me in the afternoon, praise me in the evening time. I shall always be with you. My goodness will overflow to all those who seek me. For I am a good God and I bestow good gifts unto my people. I am the I am I am good to all who seek me. I am revealing my mighty secrets unto those who diligently seek me with all their hearts.

My son come and taste and see that I am good. I am giving you all the unfailing love and mercy that I gave my servant David. Nations will come to obey you not because of your own power or virtue but because I have glorified you. My thoughts are higher than your thoughts, my ways are better than your ways. My word through you will always produce fruit, it will accomplish all I want it to, to prosper everywhere I send it. You will live in joy and peace. The miracle of growth will make the Lord's name great. At this time Gentiles will be blessed also of the Lord. They will not be second class citizens. I will bring them to my Holy mountain of Jerusalem and make them Full of joy within my House of Prayer. Tell my people that righteousness and good works although necessary will not save them, only a spirit of love committed in total surrender to me and trusting me in all things. There is no peace for that one who rejects me. A new platform do I give you, stand on it because from there you will affect many people who are now ready to receive your insights and revelation. Remember you did not come into this world to be served... but to serve. Avad!

CONTACT INFORMATION
Telephone: 563-242-9016
Fax: 563-242-5227
Email: victorycenter@qwestoffice.net
Webpage: www.victorycenter.com

REV. RAY GIMENEZ
jeremiah3117@yahoo.com
To donate for our homeless shelters go to our
webpage